The Joyous Recovery

The Joyous Recovery

A New Approach to
Emotional Healing and Wellness

Peak Living Network Book 1

The quotation from Bernie Siegel on pg. 243 is from his book *Love, Medicine, and Miracles*, HarperPerennial.

Author photo by Patrice Lenowitz

Book and cover design by Jenny Goldberg

Peak Living Network Books
PeakLivingNetwork@juno.com
PeakLivingNetwork.org

For Fabienne and Liam

Acknowledgments

Above all, I am eager to thank the people who've been my key supports during more than two years of work on this project, and during the years leading up to it: Patrice Lenowitz, John Maher, Flip Rosenberry, Daniel Ritchie, Fabienne Andrews-Lafont, Liam Andrews-Bancroft, Jay Silverman, Carlene Pavlos, and Angie Gregory. Thank you so much for your love, encouragement, and belief in me.

My tremendous gratitude to my healing partners and mentors over a period of decades: Daniel Moss, Kathleen Gambino Labb, Susie Smith, Lisa Orlando, Karen Brandow (who has passed on), Charles Convis, Lane Bennett , Dominic Kulik, David Yaskulka, Andrea Walter, Nancy Kline, Scott Darling, Pat Howe, and Jessica Zane.

My appreciation also goes out to Kathy Jones and my siblings Margery, Kate, and Tim. Also a warm thank you to Florence Bancroft, Stacy Bancroft, and Kim Tulecke Beyer for being out there inspiring me.

Huge thanks are due to Lenore Pfutzner for her meticulous and brilliant copy-editing of the book. You are reading a book that is vastly improved because of Lenore's dedicated and caring work.

My deep appreciation goes out to Jenny Goldberg for her hard work and artist's eye in designing the book and the cover, and for her patience in dealing with me as we went over the book page by page.

For inspiration: Doomtree, Mercedes Sosa, Little Simz, State Radio/Dispatch, Eddie Arjun, TV on the Radio.

Attention!
Key Information About Using This Book

This book was written to be used, not just read. Accordingly, an extensive collection of exercises accompany this book and are available free at PeakLivingNetwork.org, under "Readings". There are exercises for each chapter of this book.

One of my central messages in the pages ahead is that healing needs to be a collective process to work well. With that in mind, I encourage you to find a **partner** to read this book and work the exercises with you. Your partner could be a friend or a relative, if one comes to mind with whom you feel comfortable sharing personally. The person could be nearby or thousands of miles away, as long as you have a way to keep in regular touch as you read. If you prefer to partner with someone who isn't part of your social life, you can find a partner through the Peak Living Network website.

If you'd like to be in a **book group** for *The Joyous Recovery*, on the website you can find a guide to starting and running a group, and to finding out if someone is already starting one near you. You'll be able to list your group on our website to help you find potential members.

You can also sign up any time to follow the Peak Living Network **blog** by going to the website and clicking on "Blog".

At the same time, you can certainly get a lot out of this book by reading it on your own. Some of the exercises don't require a partner, and the concepts can benefit you immediately.

This book also serves an additional function: when you've finished it, you'll be fully prepared to be an excellent member and contributor in the Peak Living Network, should you choose to get involved with us. Toward that end, I encourage you not to skip chapters that you don't feel apply to you; the goal is for us all to get more effective at helping each other, not just at helping ourselves.

Contents

Chapter 1

The Joyous Path to Emotional Healing

Healing shouldn't have to be so hard.

I often hear versions of the following comments, made with strained voices:

"I have some really heavy issues I need to work on some day."

"There are things about myself that I avoid facing up to."

"Eventually I'm going to have to dive in and deal with all this bad stuff I went through, but I just don't want to look at that stuff."

"I'm working really hard on myself. Some things are getting better, but it's so hard to keep moving forward."

The messages that come through are:

"Emotional healing is painful, scary, and slow."

"There can be rewards eventually from healing, but first there is huge work and sacrifice, and then maybe the improvements start."

"Big changes aren't that common, but if you really put your nose to the grindstone, you'll be able to make your life better in some small ways, and that's better than nothing. Part of maturing is accepting the fact that life is hard and you need to adapt to lower expectations."

But it doesn't have to be this way.

The reason most people find healing so hard is that they've had so little help, so little guidance, and so little information. Emotional recovery can be, and should be, a joyous journey. People who get the right pieces in place find that:

- healing moves fast.

- some gains are immediate, with many more to follow.

- the pleasure greatly outweighs the pain.

- the parts that do involve hard work are so rewarding that the underlying feeling remains, *"I can totally do this."*

- healing is not a solitary undertaking, and it leads rapidly to greater and greater connection.

Some Key Internal Messages That Get in the Way

Part of what makes it hard to commit to a healing process is that we battle with one or more of the following messages:

1. "It's different for me because the things that have happened in my life are just too deep and awful."

And hand-in-hand with this message is the one that goes:

"Other people may be able to heal, but I'm way too messed up. It's too late for me."

But if you're still alive, there's still time. You can gain back a vibrant, connected, satisfying life. Pain, anxiety, and isolation do not need to dominate.

Everyone that I have ever spoken with has been through experiences, especially in childhood, that were so emotionally wrenching that it's miraculous their hearts didn't just stop beating from the pain. Even people from the kindest families and the safest towns have stunning stories to tell of heartbreak, loss, and fear.

Are there people who have had it even worse than the rest? Absolutely. Some childhoods could only be described as torture. Some people live as literal slaves. Some people have been targets of a level of cruelty that I cannot fully wrap my head around. But you know what? Somehow, seeming to defy possibility, a remarkable number of them find their way back to love and peace, back to a life that is full of meaning. The differences in how we've been hurt do matter, but they don't have to set us apart from each other. And everyone can heal.

2. "I've read so many books, I've tried so many healing approaches, I've thought and thought and thought, I've wept and wept. There's just no way out for me."

Most books about psychology and self-help are long on analyzing what we're doing wrong, especially the supposed errors in our thinking, and short on what to do about it. Their advice tends to come down to slogans like, "Change your outlook," "Think positively," and "Just do it."

It's emotional healing by bumper sticker. You end up keeping a constant eye on yourself to make sure you aren't thinking the wrong thoughts, and it becomes another way to feel like it's all your own fault.

The therapy field offers a much stronger analysis of how we get hurt than of how we heal. There are some alternative therapies, especially a genre known as "body-centered therapy," that are showing some promising healing power. But it's hard to find the depth of positive effect that we're all craving.

And there is even less information available about how to love the process of healing rather than experiencing it as a chore.

3. "This is just the way life is. Life is hard. We came into the world alone and we leave it alone. Accept it."

We "come into the world alone"? What statement could be more preposterous? We come into the world *literally inside of the body of another human being—our mother—beginning as an actual part of her*. We then go through a very gradual process of separating into an individual that can survive outside of our mother's body. And even after we're born, years go by before we are capable of surviving without almost constant assistance from other human beings. **How could we possibly come into the world less alone than we do?**

As for dying alone, we manage to avoid that for the vast majority of the human race. Most people are accompanied by one or more of their loved ones when they pass on. (And people who have come back from near-death experiences report that they went into a realm where they felt the most completely connected that they ever had!)

As for life "just being hard," I know many, many people all over the world who enjoy their lives immensely, whose pleasure and fulfillment greatly outweigh their pain. My own life has been terrific for almost two decades. Persistent suffering is not etched into the nature of being.

Look at wild animals. Do they seem to spend most of their lives suffering? No. Certainly parts of their lives are painful, but mostly they seem to do quite well. Why would the human being be the only animal destined to spend most of its life in pain?

4. "Life could never be happy all the time. There will always be pain and suffering."

True, but so what? We don't *need* to be happy all the time, and we don't need lives that are pain-free. We need lives where the happy times outweigh the sad ones; where we live with meaning and purpose; and where we feel connected to the human race, to all that lives, and to all that exists. When our days contain these elements we feel *fulfilled*, and fulfillment is what we're really wanting. And this we absolutely can have.

A New Approach

So what's different about *The Joyous Recovery*? What is this path to healing that says that you don't have to slog through your deep issues, that you don't have to "face up" to dark awful truths, and that you don't have to stew in your faults and "work on yourself" to fix what's wrong?

Here are the five key points that make the Peak Living Network approach distinct:

Point 1: We're In This Together

The Joyous Recovery is not a self-help book. In fact, the entire concept of "self-help" is mistaken. Not only does your recovery not have to be a solitary project, the reality is that it can't be; healing on your own will only move you small distances. This is why consumers of self-help literature keep thinking they've found the answer but it slips away. Emotional healing is *collective*. Either we heal in large numbers or we don't heal much at all.

Human beings are not mountain lions. Throughout almost the entirety of human history, we have been born into tribes and clans where our membership was secure from the moment we emerged into the world. We are a species of animal that watches over each other, that shares food, that sleeps piled together, that cares for the sick, that gathers for weddings and funerals. It is only in the last 3% of our history that we have *not* lived in this manner, and this means that the need and desire to live in community is programmed into us at the deepest levels.[1]

The reason we are longing for connection is that we were built to live connected.

Much of why we are feeling so wounded and unhappy is because of ways that connection in our lives broke down. Either the people who were supposed to be keeping us well were hurting us instead, or there just wasn't anyone focusing much on our wellness. *Since aloneness is one of the most profound sources of our injuries—perhaps the single most profound source—it's not surprising that we don't heal well alone.*

Try, then, to stop dumping on yourself about the resolutions you haven't been able to stick with, the diets you haven't stayed on, the exercise programs you've dropped. You aren't a weak person; you just need a team behind you. We all do.

While writing *The Joyous Recovery*, I have simultaneously launched the Peak Living Network (PLN). PLN is a free global network for anyone who chooses to be part of it. Our mission is to support each other's healing and recovery in thoughtful, aware, successful ways.

---

[1] Humans are in no way the only animal this is true of. To pick just one example, elephants are known to gather in large groups to share births and deaths.

The Peak Living Network is here to support your healing. Through the network and our website you can find, *entirely free*:

- peer-led support groups

- peer-led discussion groups

- articles and brochures

- a discussion forum about healing

- people to meet with for one-on-one support sessions (explained in Chapters 9-12)

For more information visit: PeakLivingNetwork.org

One of the core activities of the Peak Living Network is "splitting time," which we also call "co-counseling." In Chapters 9-12, I explain how to work with a partner to do healing sessions where you split the time in half; one person is the speaker during the first half while the other person listens and gives support, and then they *switch roles* for the second half of the time. Learning how to split time skillfully and effectively is a lifetime learning process; the better you get at it, the more you'll be amazed by its power to transform your life.

Structured Support

The process of splitting time illustrates one of the most important principles that distinguishes the Peak Living Network approach. Not only does healing need to be a collective process, it needs substantial parts of that support to be *structured*, so that it happens at set times of the day or the week, is planned, and follows a clear format. You'll learn many ways to apply this crucial concept in the chapters ahead and in the accompanying exercises.

Point 2: You Aren't Broken, So You Don't Need to Be Fixed

There's a big difference between saying:

"I need to change the things that are wrong with me,"

and saying:

"I choose to heal so that I can enjoy my life deeply and help those around me to do the same."

What do our emotional struggles typically look like? Mostly things like:

- being downhearted much of the time

- having low energy or low motivation

- feeling ashamed or embarrassed about who we are

- feeling unattractive or unappealing

- feeling plagued by guilt over things we've done in the past

- believing we aren't very smart

- feeling afraid, feeling limited in what we can do because of our fears

- feeling unpleasantly full of anger, feeling a lot of frustrated rage

- feeling powerless to defend ourselves or our loved ones from injustices

- feeling powerless to stop behaving in ways that are harmful to us

This list doesn't cover everything, but most of what we go through fits in here somewhere. These elements are all signs of ways in which we've been *hurt*; they are the effects of traumatic emotional injury. In most cases they are the products of wounds that happened *over and over again*, especially during childhood.

Moreover, these effects didn't come from small things. They grew out of experiences that were devastating to us when they happened, though we may have forgotten them or forgotten how bad they were.

It isn't your fault that you developed distressing effects from outrages and heartbreaks. *We all need to stop blaming ourselves, and each other, for the injuries we are carrying.*

Human healing happens most powerfully when we feel connected to our strengths. If from the outset we're made to feel that we need a repair job, how will we able to focus on what we do well and what our gifts are?

I'm not saying that positive thinking is the solution; its power has actually been greatly exaggerated. We need space to feel how bad we really feel, and not to be constantly pressured to "look on the bright side" and walk around pretending that everything is okay.

But the thing is, on a deeper level you are okay. So I'm going to encourage you to do a balancing act, where you:

- keep one foot delicately placed in the realities of today's challenges.

- keep the other foot rooted in the profound truth of who you really are.

And who you really are is the same person you were when you were born: loving, open, full of energy, and with a vast capacity for intelligence.

Point 3: To Give Is to Receive

If you go see a therapist, the discussion is all about you. The therapist doesn't open up about his or her own challenges, and you aren't expected to give anything back emotionally. In some ways this is nice; you probably don't get listened to anywhere else in your life with this kind of focused attention, and that support allows some new things to happen inside you.

But at the same time, something is a little wrong here. A message is being sent (usually not intentionally) that says, "Some people in the world are helpers, and other people are in need of help. You are one of the ones who need help. The therapist has special healing knowledge and powers that you don't."

What works better is to set up a healing path where, from the very start, we remember that we have as much to give as to receive. And I mean now; it doesn't make sense to wait "until I get it together enough to be able to offer something to other people." *Our own healing is accelerated when we contribute to the healing of others*, because:

- it helps us to see who we really are: smart, capable people with a lot to give, not helpless people who need to be endlessly rescued.

- when we help strengthen the people around us, their increased wellness then comes back to help us; we're helping them become *better helpers for us.*

- it helps us to heal injuries we carry from times when we didn't get to *give* enough caring, not just times when we didn't *receive* enough caring.

The last point above never gets mentioned. We don't just get hurt by not getting the love we need; we get just as wounded from not having the opportunity to *give* the love that we feel in our hearts, to have that love valued and treasured, and to see our love *make a difference*.

Are You Giving Too Much Already?

Perhaps you're already a generous person and you're feeling burnt out on listening to other people, attending to their needs, and helping them with their problems. You may feel that the last thing you need for your healing is to be giving even more to others. And in a sense you're right.

But I'm going to teach you a new way of giving—with some specific structures in place—that doesn't drain you. In fact, it will leave you feeling more filled up than you did without it. The difference is that we're going to set things up so that:

- you get reminded often of how much your gifts are appreciated.

- the people you are supporting are actually *moving* in their lives. That relieves you of the burden of holding people up through struggles that never seem to improve much.

- equal exchange is built into how we do things, so that you receive support in equal measure to how you give it.

Point 4: "Just Do It" Doesn't Do It—Healing is a Cycle

If we could "just do it," we would. If New Year's resolutions worked we'd all be physically fit, caught up with our taxes, out of debt, and racing forward on that novel we said we'd write some day.

At the same time, it is true that it doesn't work to keep waiting until we "feel ready" to make the changes that we hunger for in our lives. It's tragically easy to wait a lifetime for the right moment to take those big risks, to run with those great ideas, to let our hearts show.

The answer is to stop seeing these two aspects of life— getting ready to take steps vs. actually taking those steps— as an either-or choice. The reality is that the two can go on simultaneously, and in fact they should. *The Joyous Recovery* teaches you how to create a rhythm that moves steadily back and forth between:

- taking decisive action in your life, moving forward, and living fully

and

- gathering support, taking time to feel and release your fear and sadness, healing, and growing

When we stop thinking of these as opposite processes that we have to choose between, we discover that a wonderful interplay is possible.

The cycle that I will be teaching you involves:

1) Increasing our awareness of our personal strengths, and drawing upon love and support from other people—in other words, building from a strong foundation

2) Taking time to feel and process our weaknesses and wounds; that whole internal landscape where we don't feel confident or strong, where we don't feel whole, where in fact we may feel profoundly shattered; and, specifically, to release that distress through crying, laughter, and other inherent emotional healing releases that we're born with

3) Taking decisive, courageous action to improve our lives, the lives of others, and the condition of our world

These aren't different "stages," a mistake that popular healing approaches often make. We need to constantly be cycling through all three, throughout our lives. **Healing is cyclical, and each part of the cycle is equally and critically important.**

Point 5: Deep Release Shoots You Forward

The last point in this section is missing from every popular healing approach yet is the single most important concept in emotional recovery. All human beings—including you and me—come into the world built to heal. Healing *emotionally*, not just physically, is literally part of our bodies' physical design, woven into how our immune system works.

Our bodies are primed to heal emotional distress through deep, prolonged, visceral releases. There is no question that these releases are inherent, because babies and children exhibit them without ever having been taught anything about them. These processes are present because they are *necessary* to us. The specific forms they take are the following:

- deep, prolonged crying and sobbing, which is primarily a healer of grief and longing

- deep trembling, usually accompanied by frightened outbursts and agitated physical movements and often accompanied by sweating, which is primarily a healer of deep fear or terror

- deep laughter, which again may be accompanied by sweating, which is primarily a healer of fear at non-terrifying levels (including embarrassment, which is a light form of fear)

- raging, generally with intense angry noises and vigorous physical movements, which is primarily a healer of anger and injustice (a critically important and healthful release, but that unfortunately gets a bad reputation because some people use it as an excuse for frightening or intimidating other people)

- yawning, often accompanied by a desire to stretch, which is a mysterious part of this process (but is clearly one of the inherent healing releases, as I will explain)

No other healing experience open to human beings has the transforming power that the inherent releases carry when they get a chance to work as deeply as they were designed to do. They are as central to lasting recovery as antibodies are to physical healing. In fact, they are biologically interwoven in many intriguing ways with the physical immune system, as I explain in PLN Book 2, *The Emotional Immune Response*.

The inherent releases are massively—and tragically—misunderstood.

One misconception is that these releases are ways of *expressing* emotion, which they aren't. We express emotion with words, songs, paintings, tones of voice, physical movements, and other channels. The inherent releases, though, exist to *heal* pain, not to express it.

Here, then, is a crucial understanding:

Expressing pain *cannot* substitute for releasing it. These two processes play important but *distinct* roles.

That's why people can express pain endlessly without getting relief from it.

A second crucial misconception is that the inherent releases just help us manage our distress. In this view vigorous exercise, for example, plays the same role as a deep sobbing cry does, since they can both create the sense of having driven our emotional pain away. But actually two very different things have happened. The exercise has made the distress *dissipate*—which can certainly be valuable—but the deep cry has actually *healed* a significant piece of the distress so that it's *gone*, discharged from our being. Dissipation and discharge are two different processes.

The releases won't usually help that much unless they go deep. That's why you may sometimes cry all night and not wake up feeling any better. Weeping won't do it. We have to relearn how to cry like babies, no holds barred, busting it all out of ourselves like an avalanche. And in order to cry this hard, we generally have to have someone holding us snugly; unless you've had a long, deep cry while being held, you've never even discovered what crying can actually do.

When you open these natural healing channels—which may take considerable work—all your other efforts towards healing and growth will seem so much easier that you'll feel that you've entered a new life. *The deepest underpinnings of the Peak Living Network are **love** and **release**.* Our inherent nature, including the natural wisdom of our bodies, leads the way.

The five tenets I've covered in this chapter put us on a healing path that is connected, successful, and deeply rewarding. There's no need to slog through a swamp in hope of reaching green lands in some distant future; the joy of regaining the pieces of ourselves that we lost, the joy of regaining our excitement and engagement with life, can begin today. So why not do it that way?

Key Points to Remember:

- Your healing doesn't need to be all up to you. Healing is a collective process.

- We're not fixing what's wrong with us, we're healing.

- We don't heal well unless we're involved with healing others, and we don't help other people well unless we're involved in our own healing. The two have to go together.

- Trying harder won't work; we need well thought-out plans that can succeed, following a proven set of steps and with adequate support and resources, including *structured* support.

- The deep releases we were born with are the greatest keys to faster and deeper emotional recovery. There is no path that heals us more profoundly.

Chapter Two

Okay, Let's Talk About It: How We Get So Hurt

You were a baby once. You were full of openness, you trusted the world, you wanted everyone to be happy. You had needs, but as long as those were met you were fine with whatever else made up the day, interested in all of it. Life enthralled you.

It's not that life was perfect. There were painful hours when your stomach was bothering you or your head felt bad, and you didn't have a way yet to tell people exactly what the problem was so they had to guess as well as they could. But at the same time, you didn't really need that much. Once the problem was solved, you were good to go.

So what went wrong?

In the chapter ahead, I'm going to explain how we get hurt and what the results are. Let me begin, though, by explaining why I'm going down this road:

Reason 1: I want you to stop blaming yourself for where you are today.

It's not that I want you to let yourself off the hook to behave in ways that aren't good for you; in fact, I'm going to be pressing you to take decisive action on a number of fronts. But I'd like you to stop putting yourself down. There are good reasons why you face the challenges you do, based on what you have come through. This is true for all of us.

Reason 2: This information will help you recognize that all people have histories that have brought them to where they are today.

I'm not talking about letting other people treat you badly; in fact, one of the messages of this book is that we all need to get better at stopping people from mistreating us. But we can stop blaming people for their own difficulties. No one was born evil or selfish. Everybody's trying to find a way to the light, even people who don't look that way at all.

Reason 3: When we're armed with an understanding of emotional injury and the harm it causes, we can start to outwit some of the unhealthy patterns we've developed.

In the long term we can't get free from our injuries by gaining more and more insight into how we got hurt; it's a dead end after a while. But in the short term, a degree of insight *does* help us to win early rounds in the fight for wellness. And winning some early rounds matters, as it helps us build a foundation that longer-term healing can grow from.

The Beginning

Babies are powerfully intuitive. In one sense they understand very little of what's going on around them, but in another way they're the ones grasping it all the most acutely. They pick up quickly on whether they are loved and wanted. They sense when those around them are tense, afraid, or despondent. They feel the quality of people's skin, and through its currents they pick up calm, stress, rage, or serenity.

Babies do not need to be in a perfect environment, though; this is a point where some confusion reigns today. A baby is fine with some level of stress in the surroundings, with some conflict between people, with a parent who is having a hard day. Ordinary, healthy human life includes these challenges. What matters for the infant is:

- that these distresses in people around them not become extreme and that people not remain in these states too long.

- that they get a clear sense of tensions resolving, of life going back to normal after the storm cloud has passed.

- that they can feel adults paying focused, caring attention to them, that people around them aren't so deeply lost in their distress that it feels like they've gone away.

Babies pick up strong impressions from their environment before they are even born. Studies have found, for example, that when a man is abusing his pregnant partner the unborn baby absorbs the stress in harmful ways.

Thus the first layer of hurt in a young child originates from absorbing the distresses of people in his or her world, mostly from times when those people are suffering or numbed out to such an extent that they can't attend to the baby's need for love, attention, and basic care.

High quality, focused attention is one of the outstanding needs that children have. They get put down for this by adults. "Oh, you're just doing that to get attention...Why can't you just be good and play on your own, can't you see that I'm busy?" We teach kids that they're bad for wanting what they deeply need.

The battle for attention is getting worse today because adults who are supposedly spending time with children are giving their attention to the screens on their phones and computers instead of being meaningfully present. The cell phone has made all interactions interruptible, with vast consequences for children (and for all of us).

―――――――――

A brief aside: I don't wish to join with modern psychology's focus on blaming parents for everything. The structure of modern life victimizes parents too. The raising of children has become an isolated job, due to the destruction of our communities. Parents are way overworked in today's economy and are scarred by old wounds of their own. At the same time, we have to speak honestly and directly about what happens to children or we can't address the injuries we carry.

―――――――――

The second layer in children's injuries enters as they begin for the first time to come under attack. Adults, and sometimes older children, start to yell at them, threaten them, tell them what their faults are, and call them insulting names. These behaviors are considered normal; just go shopping and you'll hear children being told:

"If you keep acting that way, you'll be sorry!"

"Stop acting like a baby! Be a big girl (big boy)."

"What's the matter with you? Why can't you think about what you're doing?"

"You better stop your crying or you're going to get it!"

Attacks on children come in a number of important forms, so I'm going to break them down:

Violence

Violence begins early in the lives of children. Much of it is euphemistically referred to as "spanking" or "physical discipline," but assault is assault. Why would it be any less traumatic for children to be physically hit—especially by loved ones—than it is for adults? Children are *more* easily scarred than adults, not less so. Most people seem to forget what it was like to get spanked, but I remember it well: the pain, the shock, and the heartbreaking betrayal of knowing that it was my mother who was hitting me.

If you've hit children in the past, forgive yourself but don't do it anymore. If you were hit when you were a child, begin to remember the toll that took on you, most of which you've probably blocked from your mind.

Children also get physically harmed and intimidated by other adults; step-parents, grandparents, school teachers, and employees of institutions (such as mental health or correctional facilities). Millions of kids witness men being violent toward their mothers. Virtually all children live with violence from bigger kids, and at times the severe fear of that violence. These child-on-child assaults originate in adult violence and are passed down through the ranks of children.

Much of the violence that children are subjected to takes the form of sexual violations and assaults. A phenomenal percentage of boys and an even higher percentage of girls are sexually abused at some point in their growing up.

Societal Violence

Finally, children are exposed to societal violence: police and military violence against civilians; war; families being thrown out of their homes and off their land; and shootings and assaults on the streets. People who are privileged may think of emotional injury as meaning "the way our families messed us up," but for huge portions of the world's population the source of harm is more outside the family than within it.

Many parents are paid so little at their jobs that they have to work an impossible number of hours per week in order to survive, and thus are forced to spend very little time with their kids. This is a form of societal violence, both toward the parent and toward the child.

Children Learn That Something is Wrong With Them

Children get the message, from various sources, that they're bad; not that they're behaving unacceptably, but that something inside them is truly rotten.

Much of the modern world sees children as inherently corrupt *from birth*, so that adults have to beat the evil—figuratively or literally—out of the child. But even adults who don't subscribe to these kinds of explicit beliefs still subject children to disgust, devastating criticism, and exaggeratedly harsh punishments that communicate unmistakably: "Something is deeply and inherently *wrong* with you." Adults forget how crushing these messages are for kids; if there is a hidden seed of evil inside of children, adults planted it there.

Inferiority

From the beginnings of consciousness, children get the message that adults are more valuable human beings and are to be taken more seriously. Childhood is viewed as *a condition to be overcome.* (Take that in for a moment.)

One of the early forms of this devaluing is when children are told to "be a big girl/big boy" and "act grown up." These statements teach kids from the outset to be ashamed of their littleness and to see being older and bigger as *better.* Without intending to, we teach kids to hate themselves for being little—and the result is that they do.

Children's inferior status leads to their being *denied a voice.* They get little or no say over the crucial decisions that determine the course of their lives. They get told to shut up when they express their opinions or lodge their objections. And if a child dares express outrage at adult cruelty, irrationality, or unfairness, the retaliation that follows can be severe and violent. *Being silenced at times of injustice is among the most painful of human experiences, and children don't feel it a drop less profoundly than adults do.*

Children Are Fully Alive

We don't view adulthood as just a stage where we're getting ready for old age, nor do we view old age as just a stage where we're preparing to be dead. So why do we treat childhood as a pre-human stage where we prepare to become adults, thereby devaluing the beauty, magic, and depth of childhood? Each stage in life is its own way of being, inherently valuable and important, not just a transition to something else.

The devaluing of children and childhood is our single most serious social problem in the modern world, the poison from which all other toxicity flows. Being taught that you are inherently inferior is the single most destructive aspect of any form of oppression; the crowning horror of them all is being taught that you are deeply, truly, *less of a person.*

Neglect

So many children are left to fend largely for themselves, starved for love, affection, and companionship. Some of them are not even fed and kept safe with any regularity. Many of our most profound but hidden scars are from not having been cared for.

And even kids whom we think of as "spoiled" aren't seen, valued, or respected; treating a child as a perfect possession, put up on a pedestal, is simply another way to erase and ignore the actual person. Being spoiled is about being given objects and privileges—things you don't need—while at the same time your true needs are ignored.

The Dismissing of Children's Feelings

Children's feelings are not taken seriously. Hardly a day goes by in the lives of children without adults (and older children) making fun of their hurts, trivializing their losses, blaming their distress on them, and threatening them for showing emotion. Children feel pain as acutely as adults do; so why is it okay to laugh at their anguish?

Consider a typical scenario: A child builds a house out of blocks, and the house gets knocked over and wrecked. The child is full of sadness and starts to wail. The adult says, "Come on, don't be silly, it's no big deal," all in a disparaging tone. The sadness of losing the house, which was already substantial for the child, has now been quadrupled by the pain of having his or her sadness ridiculed.

In a disturbing twist, children are also laughed at for their joy and excitement, for the intensity of their love for other people or for animals, for their pride in themselves. The dismissal of their *positive* emotions is part of teaching kids that they don't matter.

The Denial of the Right to Heal

Children are permitted little release of emotion, which as we will see is the key to emotional healing. Children's crying is virtually forbidden by the adult world, as are most of their efforts to release anger and frustration, fear, and anxiety. Children thereby lose the lion's share of their opportunity to genuinely heal the painful losses and attacks they've endured, and instead are forced to "adapt" and "be resilient."

Once in a while I see adults grasp the size of a child's loss—when a parent has died for example—but this is more the exception than the rule.

Isolation

The greatest source of children's isolation is the gradual and devastating global destruction of communities. Until recent times, children spent their days surrounded by other children. But now they have largely lost access to each other; they spend much of their time with just their siblings, or alone with adults. The main reason why adults put young kids in front of videos is that those children don't have anyone to play with.

Children also used to have more adults in their lives, particularly their aunts and uncles, grandparents, and other relatives. In historical terms it is only recently that people stopped living in tribes or clans, taking collective responsibility for the care of the children; kids felt that a world of adults—and older children—watched over them.

Children are around other kids at school, but one of the primary goals of schools is to *prevent them from interacting with each other*. They spend a small portion of the day getting to play or talk.

The result is that children are lonely. They learn to numb out this loneliness through the use of screens, including their phones. But numbing a feeling doesn't keep it from being a dominant force in life; in fact, we're more controlled by the painful feelings we block than by the ones we feel.

Isolation is deliberately used as a way to force a child to stop crying; "If you're going to be that way, you have to do it in your room." Being isolated will, over time, stop up a child's crying channel as effectively as outright intimidation will.

Hierarchy

Modern society is built on a system of hierarchies. Every inch of our lives is structured into divisions between people who are treated as more valuable and less valuable, who do more of the unpleasant work and less of the unpleasant work, who have more wealth and who have less wealth, who have all the say and who have none of the say. Hierarchy works well for chickens but it is devastating for human beings. When you're a child you may be looked down upon not only for being a kid, but also for being a person of color, a female, a person with a disability, or a child of parents who work with their hands. Your oppression as a child is the *template* for many other forms of oppression into which you are socialized.

Modern healing systems make almost no mention of oppression, leaving out one of the most urgent issues we have to process in order to heal well. (See Chapter 18.)

Locks on the Escape Exit

There are two kinds of childhood injury that play a special role because of the way they get piled on top of other wounds and act as *locks*, deepening what we've already suffered and making it harder to climb out from under it all.

The first kind is *being taught that we caused what happened to us*. Children get told everything from, "The reason you don't have any friends is because you're selfish," to, "Your mother died because your behavior caused her so much stress." You were not to blame for *any* of what was done to you, as will be a central theme in our work ahead.

The second kind is enduring terrible events and *having people around us act as if nothing happened*. This failure of the world to respond is a factor in the blocking of traumatic memories; when no one notices, and there is no one the child can safely tell, the memory of the event gets buried in unmentionable pain.

The non-response causes us to doubt our grip on reality, leading us to feel that:

- we must have imagined the events.

- the world must approve of what happened to us.

- we must have deserved it.

- we must be overreacting.

- the world is a cold, uncaring place.

These beliefs about life creep into all of us in the wake of the traumatic experiences we were left to deal with alone.

A closing point: We have common ground with every person in our world, for we are all either children or survivors of childhood.

How Injury Manifests Itself

1. Pervasive and Intermittent Distress

The first and most obvious effect of unhealed emotional injury is that pain becomes *pervasive*; we come to spend a lot of our lives hurting about things. We know we're dealing with unhealed wounds when:

- the pain continues years after the event.

- we hurt about issues that don't look that painful on the surface, indicating that the pain is connected to something *else*, usually from earlier in life.

- we struggle with general downheartedness that has no clear source (sometimes labeled "depression").

- we have emotional reactions that make no sense to us, such as feeling a wave of sadness or fear when an exciting positive event occurs.

- life comes to feel *hard*; we feel the weight of it in our posture, in the droop of our heads, in our reluctance to get out of bed in the morning, in our dark philosophies about life.

We also face *intermittent* distress, commonly referred to as "getting triggered" or "having your buttons pushed." A trigger can be something as simple as a sound or a smell, or as complex as an hour-long debate with a friend or partner. The sign of being triggered is that you feel a rush of emotion out of proportion to, or unrelated to, what just happened. A certain aroma in a stairway can bring on a wave of sadness; the sound of music playing in the distance can make you miss someone you haven't thought about for a long time.

Learning to recognize when we're triggered, and developing constructive responses to those moments, can in itself help us live better. Make it part of your daily habits to:

- check in with yourself frequently to notice what you're feeling.

- when you're feeling upset or uncomfortable ask yourself, "What does the current scene connect to from earlier times in my life?"

- ask yourself, "Do my feelings seem bigger right now than would fit the present issue?"

Don't allow this effort to throw you off kilter, though. I've seen people become *too* questioning of their present feelings, constantly doubting the validity of their reactions to events.

2. Numbing Out

The next effect is that we *shut down*. There are times in life, especially in childhood, when our pain literally becomes greater than our organism can endure. In order to stay alive, we are forced to block the crushing pain, and the only way to do so is to *close down portions of ourselves*. Through this process we gradually lose the lion's share of our capabilities, not only of our ability to think clearly and solve problems but also of our ability to feel joy, to be full of energy, and to love one another.

Those pieces aren't truly dead, because they can live again. When you engage in deep healing you'll find that you keep unearthing parts of yourself that feel like deeply treasured old friends.

In day-to-day life, we experience the effects of shut-down as *numbness*. People in our times crave to feel things more, to be more affected by a beautiful view, a loving interaction, or exciting good news. Perhaps the single most common complaint in modern life is that time is going by too fast. Life is actually very, very long; but numbness can cause it to slip away.

The way to slow down the rush of the years is to experience deep healing. Doing so allows us to engage fully again with our bodies, our senses, and our emotions. The years return to being rich and fulfilling, and a lifetime once again feels like enough time.

3. The Toll on our Bodies

Our emotional wounds get encoded in our bodies, contributing to chronic pain, disease, and physical rigidities.[1] Current physical experiences (injuries, intense pleasure, deep massage) can awaken memories that appear to have been stored in a specific body part. Our efforts to overcome these difficulties through stretching, yoga, or physical therapy progress more rapidly when we also attend to healing our emotional wounds.

[1] See *The Body Keeps the Score* by Bessel van der Kolk

Unfolding Rather Than Changing

Understanding this morass of injuries and their lasting effects leads us to one of the most important concepts of the Peak Living Network outlook:

When we deeply grasp what has happened to us, it becomes clear that *we're doing great.*

One of the essential shifts in perspective that I'm hoping you'll take from *The Joyous Recovery* is to drop the notion, "I need to change what's wrong with me," and replace it with, *"It's incredible that I've done as well as I have. Now it's time to do even better."*

Think of healing not as a process of changing, but the opposite: of *becoming more truly the person you've always been.* It's about going back along the road picking up all the pieces of yourself that were taken from you along the way. We're not trying to fix what's wrong with you; we're trying to set what's right with you free.

Awareness is Uncomfortable

Since traumatic injury leads to loss of awareness, it naturally follows that the healing process brings about an *expansion* of awareness. This opening is wonderful but comes with its own set of challenges; saying good-bye to numbness means entering into a less comfortable life. Our emotional life becomes vibrant, which is more satisfying but also unsettling.

We don't need to pull back from this growing awareness. We can create a healing process that is sustainable; you'll be learning how in the chapters ahead. Healing leads to more awareness which in turn leads to more healing, a wonderful cycle that makes life exciting, fulfilling, and at times exhilarating. We come to welcome discomfort and upheaval rather than ducking away from it.

The pursuit of comfort has, mistakenly, become the dominant goal of modern life. When we pursue ease above all else, we end up abandoning our deeper craving for a life that is *fulfilling* and *connected*. Avoiding discomfort stops being so important to us once we've tasted how satisfying a well-lived life can feel.

Why It's Hard When Things Go Well

"I'm falling crazy in love with someone. Why do I feel ill?"

"I just got offered a job that I've dreamed of for a decade. Why am I dying to scream and tell them I don't want it?"

Good news can, oddly, make us feel bad. Why do we get scared when things improve in our lives? Why do we sometimes sabotage ourselves, making a mess of things right when life was looking up?

The answer is largely unrecognized: *Positive experiences can trigger old emotional injuries just as powerfully as negative ones do*. Being flooded by fear, sadness, or anxiety is a natural and common reaction to major positive life events.

One reason why this happens is that our inner being is trying to heal. We heal best in our *strongest* moments, not when we're deep in discouragement or isolation. So when our intuition perceives sources of strength or excitement arriving in our lives, it seizes that opportunity to try to dump some of the old distress we're carrying around; it assumes we're ready to handle it. As we'll see, this is a healing opportunity.

There are various additional reasons why we get triggered when we start to feel good:

People in the past didn't want us to do well. You may have grown up in a family or neighborhood where there was nasty competitiveness, envy, and back stabbing. Whenever you started to seem happy or successful, people targeted you for insults and put-downs or they cut you off. So now any time you do well you feel like you're about to get attacked.

We were made to feel that we didn't deserve good things. You may have grown up with guilt being dumped on you, perhaps being taught that it's unfair for you to do well while other people are suffering. (For example, I've watched some depressed parents criticize their kids for acting too happy or energetic.) The result is that now you feel like you're abandoning other people if you don't stay down in their hole with them.

We feel that we'll destroy it. You may have grown up subjected to messages that you can't do anything right, that you don't try hard enough, or that you're stupid. So success is scary because you're convinced that you're going to mess everything up soon and ruin your triumph.

We feel that we can't withstand any more losses. It can feel safer to live with steady low-level dissatisfaction than to go big for what you really want and risk the heartbreak of having it taken away later.

Being happy feels like giving up on healing. Many of us carry an unconscious fear that if our lives go well in the present we'll lose the chance to ever work through the bad stuff from earlier. Sometimes it takes the form of feeling that, if we're seen as successful, no one will ever acknowledge how horrible or unjust the bad parts of the past were.

Be patient with yourself about reacting negatively to positive events. It's a natural reaction to past wounds, and you'll learn how to keep it from stopping you.

Longing

Are you familiar with k.d. lang's beautiful voice singing, "Constant craving has always been"? She's capturing a powerful aspect of our experience. But life hasn't actually always been that way, and it certainly doesn't need to stay that way now. A huge proportion of what we long for today actually has nothing to do with the present. We are feeling hungry for what we didn't get—but desperately needed—long ago. **The endless and largely unaware effort to get today what we failed to get long ago actually keeps us from getting what we need today.**

Consider this illustration:

Marci meets Zander and falls head-over-heels in love; he seems to be everything she hoped for in a partner. But a year or so into their relationship she starts to feel bad as Zander becomes less and less connected. He goes off into his own world, spends more time with his friends than with her, and avoids the deeper topics that he and Marci used to talk about.

Two years later, nothing has changed. Zander is still a kind, good guy, but he's not really there anymore except in brief spurts. Marci gets her hopes up and gets them dashed, over and over again. But she can't bear to end the relationship because those early months were so amazing.

When Marci fell in love with Zander, something happened that is rampant when relationships are new: she started to feel unconsciously that his love was going to fill up all the empty places she had accumulated over her lifetime. But it turned out that the relationship not only couldn't do that—*no* relationship could—it couldn't even meet her present needs.

So why can't she leave? Because she is deeply in the grip of those early hopes. A lifetime's worth of longing got rolled up into one big ball. We've all had experiences that trigger our entire history of empty parts in this way.

The reality, though, is that no experience can meet our lifetime of unmet needs. *We can only get today what we need today*—or perhaps as far back as last week or last month at the most. Unmet needs from further back than that are *frozen* inside of us. They *cannot be filled*, and we'll keep harming our lives with our attempts to do so. But they *can be healed*; and they can heal thoroughly, as any emotional wound can.

Frozen needs can cause our lives to be largely about longing. We long for our next vacation, we long for loved ones who have passed away, we long to fall in love. Our longings show up in mysterious dissatisfactions, like when we're with people we love but we feel lonely. We eat lots of sweets or drink too much alcohol or become obsessive about exercise because we're trying to fill a void from long ago.

The good news is that frozen needs can heal the same way any emotional wound does, following the steps you'll learn ahead.

Closeness Becomes Difficult

Our accumulated distress can keep us apart from each other, making it hard for us to sustain close relationships in a number of ways:

- Because we've been seriously hurt by people we loved, we experience closeness as dangerous. Much of what isn't working in our connections with each other has roots in the fear that we will be betrayed, invaded, devalued, or dominated.

- Old injuries magnify mistakes that people in our lives make. When a loved one acts distracted, selfish, or critical, our hurt gets sharpened by wounds that are triggered. And when we're caught in this wave of reactivity it's hard to work through conflicts.

- We come into our relationships carrying starvation and desperation from the past. Frozen needs inside both people sometimes make it impossible for either of them to feel satisfied.

- Most of us have suffered repeated assaults on our self-opinion, so we start human connections unconsciously feeling, "They won't like me once they really get to know me."

- Accumulated injury takes a bite out of people's ability to listen to each other. Even some people who consider themselves great listeners aren't really hearing. Overcoming blocks to truly listening to each other is a major theme of *The Joyous Recovery*.

Thus we all need to be involved in healing in order to find our way back to each other.

What It All Adds Up To

Looking at all these effects together brings us to one of the central tenets of the Peak Living Network: **Chronic human difficulties have their roots in ways we've been emotionally wounded and never got the chance to heal.**

We've all had so much mistreatment, neglect, and isolation piled on us that in our present form we're just a fraction of what our fullness really is. We are largely stuck in the deep past, my ancient self at war with your ancient self, when in the present moment we belong on the same team. We are great people with a deep capacity to love each other and love life. We're just *wounded*.

Regaining Flexibility

As you go up the food chain toward beings of greater complexity you also find increasing flexibility. The simpler forms of life operate largely from instinct, a limited set of behavioral options. As animals evolve they rely less on instinct and in its place develop *flexible thinking*, including *creativity*. Instead of just selecting behaviors from a menu, the animal becomes more able to design a new response that uniquely fits the current challenge. At the level of animals like elephants, porpoises, apes, and humans, instinct starts to play a small role, with our primary reliance being on highly flexible intelligence.

So when we become *in*flexible in our thinking and behavior, that's a sign of a place we've been wounded.

The rigidities we develop are called "behavior patterns" or simply "patterns," because we behave *repetitively* and inflexibly in ways that aren't good for us or that harm people around us. Rigidities damage relationships, as when someone just has to have things be a specific way or when there are certain subjects you can't bring up with them because they react so irrationally.

One of the wonderful effects of emotional healing is that we see our flexibility coming back to us. As attached as we may be to our rigidities, escaping them ends up feeling like breaking out of a cage; we're actually dying to shake free of them.

We Developed Patterns for Survival

How do we get through our darkest times, especially during childhood when we're so vulnerable?

- We learn to escape the toxicity by going into our own world, or training ourselves not to care, or developing self-numbing strategies such as overeating or substance abuse.

- We learn to harm ourselves physically, because physical pain blocks out intolerable emotional pain.

- We learn to create tension and drama in our lives, either because that's the only way to get any attention when we're little or because we need to divert our family from the things they're doing to each other.

This list of survival patterns could go on and on.

The fact that we developed these patterns is nothing to be ashamed of. At the time they were creative and strong forms of resistance (yes!) to what was going on in our lives. In the context of the crises in which they arose, they did far more good than harm. *We wouldn't be here today if we hadn't developed these patterns*; we would have either died or completely broken apart spiritually, ending up talking to imaginary people or in some other state of severe mental breakdown.

In the Peak Living Network we strive to avoid referring to patterns as signs of immaturity, proof of an unhealthy need to protect our ego, or evidence of our unrealistic outlook. They are evidence of what it took to survive.

At the same time, these patterns take on a life of their own and they don't go away spontaneously. In the present we can see that they've outlived their usefulness and now are limiting us and causing harm.

Recognizing Flip Sides

Patterns have opposites. Let's say that the children in a family are suffering because one of their parents is alcoholic. The siblings head in different directions; one child eventually becomes alcoholic herself, while another child becomes dogmatically anti-alcohol and judgmental of anyone who drinks. These two outcomes are flip sides of the same pattern, two flavors of rigidity growing from the same injuries.

It's tempting to flip a pattern over. If you realize, for example, that you've been sexually repressed all your life, you may react by going through a phase where you sleep with almost anyone. But the flip side of a pattern ends up causing serious problems just as the original pattern did. (Hence the saying, "The opposite of dysfunction is dysfunction.")

We don't want to just replace a rigidity with a better rigidity, though that can sometimes be helpful as a *short-term* strategy; the long-term goal is to *escape* rigidity, moving into flexibly clear thinking and conscious choices.

Healthy disciplines are not the same as rigidities. The sign that we're dealing with a rigidity is when we get bent out of shape if we can't follow our routines for a day or a week, or when we follow routines that:

- aren't good for us, such as requiring our morning cup of coffee in order to function.

- harm our connectedness, such as missing a key social event because we haven't run our daily ten miles yet.

- make us unhappy, such as feeling compelled to follow certain ritual behaviors that we find tedious or tiring.

Societal Patterns

An indispensable understanding about emotional injury is absent from the mainstream of psychological thinking:

We carry huge negative effects from the unhealthful aspects of our societies.

In fact, these are the greatest causes of our emotional wounds. Psychologists and self-help writers blame everything on families, ignoring the vast impact of:

1) Systemic oppression, including institutionalized class oppression, sexism, racism, and adultism (see Chapter 18)

2) Various additional destructive aspects of our societies and cultures

In the modern world, we absorb our cultures through, for example:

- music videos, television, and movies

- laws, and the actions of police and courts

- news media

- religion

- societal messages about right and wrong, boys vs. girls, nature vs. "progress," and countless other values

Mainstream U.S. culture, for example, teaches that:

- men get to blame their violence on women.

- alcohol abuse is completely normal until it reaches extreme consequences.

- the path to happiness is through the buying, owning, and using of objects.

In other words, our patterns are shaped by *falsehoods*, some of which come from individuals but many of which are inculcated and accepted by the wider society. It doesn't work to interpret all destructive behaviors as coming from a person's private wounds.

"Mental Illness"

There's no clear line between people who are ill and those who are well, nor is there any consensus about the definition of emotional wellness. I see people all over the U.S. who are full of irrational hatred, violence, and bigotry, but whom other people consider great leaders. In fact when you research the history of which people have been declared "mentally ill," you find that they are largely people who refused to shut up about injustice, not the people causing that injustice.

When you learn the histories of people who have become non-functioning—people who hear tormenting voices, or who can't tell fantasy from reality, or who have lost all control over their impulses—you end up hearing of abuse and cruelty at a level that's hard to fathom.

Furthermore, some of what we think of as the effects of mental illness are actually *effects of psychiatric medications*. And, ironically, one of the common side effects can be the worsening of the mental health symptoms over time.[2]

The Peak Living Network is a place where all people are welcome, and we reject the stigma of "a history of mental illness." We support people to make their own decisions about their medications, respecting what they decide is best for them.

Moving Forward

Understanding our emotional injuries, and the behavior patterns that result from them, helps us to understand what's happening in our lives, stop blaming ourselves, and stop blaming each other. You are not to blame for the difficulties you're in. Your emotional distresses have a history. Your patterns developed in response to severe emotional crises and were valuable at that time, even though they are now in your way.

Everyone around you is walking wounded as well.

Given our histories, we are doing remarkably well. We wish to do better in the future—and we will—but to get

---

[2] Although "chemical imbalances" are often stated as fact, no such imbalances have been persuasively found in research. Furthermore, long-term use of psychiatric medication has been shown to lead to numerous difficulties, For a review of the research on both of these points see *Anatomy of an Epidemic* by Robert Whitaker.

there we first have to notice the stunning accomplishments it took to get us where we are today. This is true for every one of us.

Based on these understandings, we need to push in directions that may feel contradictory at first. Let's reach simultaneously to:

become more forgiving toward ourselves
- and -
hold ourselves to higher and higher standards

become more understanding about other people's difficulties
- and -
become more and more firm about how they're allowed to treat us

deepen our understanding of how our pasts have harmed and limited us
- and -
strive to use that less and less as an excuse, focusing less and less of our attention there

These are tricky challenges, but you'll develop an intuitive feeling for how they lead to progress.

I've equipped you with the essential information you need about emotional injury. Now begins the dance of emotional healing and the reclaiming of our lives.

Part One

How Healing Begins

Chapter Three

The Elements of Emotional Healing

Recovery is not vague and mysterious. We know where it comes from, and we know what it takes to get our healing processes functioning. The Peak Living Network exists to empower all of us to take charge of our own healing, and to share the resources needed to make our recovery successful. This chapter gives an overview of the PLN approach and is a blueprint for the rest of the book.

There are a few important points to explain before I dive in:

- These elements are not steps. They don't take place in any order. And none of them is more important than the others, with the possible exception of "structured support" and "the inherent emotional releases" (numbers two and six below).

- Our healing zips forward when we get a rhythm going among *all* these elements, like the different instruments in a band playing beautiful music together. Any of them may take brief rests, but we want to keep them all moving most of the time.

- There are many important ways that we learn to manage our injuries and to work around them, and the passage of time often makes memories less painful. But these are examples of coping, which is different from truly healing.

- You'll recognize some of the elements below from other healing systems. But the problem is that they don't work well unless they're all present. Any of these elements in the absence of the others either stops helping very much (as happens with insight) or simply stops functioning (as happens with crying).

1. Remember and Understand What Has Taken Place

As I discussed in the last chapter, memory and insight are beginning pieces for each new wave of healing we experience. As you work through the exercises that accompany this book, your memories of certain events or times will become clearer, and you may remember events that you had entirely forgotten. Our injuries are often mixed up with falsehoods we were told (such as being told that what happened was our own fault or was "natural"). Gaining accurate information is powerful, and reclaiming our memories is part of reclaiming ourselves.

2. Reforge Connectedness

Unhealed emotional injuries pull us away from ourselves, from each other, and from our communities. There is a crucial two-way street in our healing processes: healing is necessary for us to be able to rebuild our connections, but rebuilding our connections is necessary for us to heal. So there needs to be a constant back-and-forth between healing and connecting. Over the course of this book and the exercises that go with it, you'll be working to deepen your relationships with other people and with yourself, reconnect with the joy and wonder of your body, and rediscover the healing power of touch.

Love is one of the greatest healing forces for the human being, perhaps the greatest of all. The Peak Living Network strives at all times to create the most loving community we can to support all of us in our healing.

One of the characteristics that most distinguishes the PLN approach is that we view healing itself as a collective process; we do most of our healing work with the active support and companionship of other people. More specifically, we build *structured support* regularly into our lives; the chapters ahead explain in detail what I mean by "structured support" and why it is *the* game-changer in emotional recovery.

3. Build from Strength

We do not need to fix ourselves because there is nothing wrong with us. We need to *heal*, which is not the same as a repair job. We're working to set what is right with us free, not to purge us of what's bad. Another way to think of it is to say that the parts we need to get rid of aren't really parts of us at all; they're more like parasites that attached themselves to us along the way, products of our injuries. Healing well requires constantly reminding ourselves and each other of our strength, our skills, and our goodness. I'll be encouraging you to keep coming around, over and over, to noticing what you have to be proud of and what you have done well so far.

4. Express the Full Truth

There is so much that we never let other people see about what our lives have been like. Indeed, there's a good deal we've never expressed even to ourselves. Coming forward with the truth involves not just telling our full stories to supportive people, but also writing in our journals, creating artwork and music, communicating the truth with our bodies, and many other channels of expression. The exercises for this book (which are at PeakLivingNetwork.org) guide you in truth-telling, which is the focus of Chapter 6.

5. Feel and Reflect

Unhealed emotional injury brings numbness and confusion. In order to heal, we have to reopen our ability to feel our feelings. Simultaneously, we need to find time and space in our lives where we can think in peace so that our heads can move toward clarity and away from all the noise, confusion, and efforts by others to control our thinking. Some of this reflecting needs to happen alone and some with other people.

6. Laugh, Cry, Storm, and Tremble

The single most crucial and powerful element of human healing is built into our bodies: the physical discharge of painful emotions through our inherent emotional release channels. These processes do not have to be taught to us; they function automatically as soon as we're born. They are, in fact, our bodies' innate plan for keeping us *emotionally* well. Tragically, these biological systems have been profoundly misunderstood and their healing power completely overlooked—despite mountains of experience *and of research* showing that they are the most powerful healing path we have open to us. In the Peak Living Network, we strive to keep these inherent emotional releases as a centerpiece of our healing work.

7. Take Action to Build the Life and the World You Want

Most popular approaches to healing fail to understand the relationship between emotional healing and taking action, usually emphasizing one way out of proportion to the other. To have a successful healing journey you need to take courageous action to improve your life, including taking action before you feel "ready" to do so. But at the same time, it is crucial that you take those leaps with careful thought and with lots of emotional support, and that those efforts *be followed by healing time*. This back and forth process is a recurring theme in the chapters ahead.

Moreover, our healing depends on us becoming increasingly able over time to take action to improve the world, not just to make life better for ourselves. We need to reclaim not just our personal power but our collective power; I have yet to encounter a widely-known healing approach that includes this indispensable element.

8. Feed Your Soul

Our hearts have needs just as our bodies do. We need to give and receive love, to have affection, to spend time in nature, to play and have fun, to be in the presence of beauty and drink it in. As we get better at identifying what we truly need—as opposed to a lot of false needs that our wounds convince us to chase (such as wealth, fame, and status)—

we become more able to fulfill our longings. And doing so in turn helps our other healing processes swing into gear.

Many healing paths catch some of these pieces. But the interplay among these elements, and how to keep that interplay working, is not understood well. Moreover, the emotional discharge piece and the structured support piece are completely missing from all the well-known approaches, yet are the most important elements of all.

In the chapters ahead, we'll explore each of these aspects of healing in detail and learn how to make them flow together. Creating harmony among these pieces is what makes healing become joyous and empowering.

Key Points to Remember:

- Emotional healing is not a mysterious process. We know concretely what needs to happen.

- You can learn how to get these different elements working beautifully together.

Chapter Four

A Surprise Beginning

I'm going to start in the opposite direction from what you may expect. Isn't the key to healing to find someone who can really listen to you? Isn't that what we all need to run out and find?

Not exactly. In fact, the search for someone who can really hear us, a listener who can absorb our whole story, ends up being a dead end. We talk and talk to each other, and to therapists, but not much healing happens. What's wrong?

These efforts aren't working because *the person speaking isn't connected enough to the person listening*. Talking doesn't lead to healing unless you have a meaningful human connection to the person you're speaking to. And you build that connection by first *listening*, not by talking.

The first step to healing, then, is to dramatically change how we listen to other people. Getting people to listen well to us comes later, and we'll return to that.

Listening: A Brief Overview

Listening well is a skill, a discipline, and an art. It is complex enough that in a lifetime we can't learn everything there is to know about it. We all need to work steadily on improving our listening throughout our lives, even those—and sometimes especially those—who believe they're already great listeners.

Here are the foundational elements of good listening:

Elements of Good Listening

- Focusing your attention—*really* focusing it—on the person speaking, while still remaining relaxed and natural

- Hearing what the person is saying

- Hearing the meaning, intentions, and emotions behind what they're saying

- Hearing what they *aren't* saying

- Responding in ways that make the person feel *heard* and *understood*, showing that you're really taking in what they've expressed

- Asking questions that draw the person out to say more

- Sorting out your own assumptions, prejudices, and needs, to prevent them from interfering with your ability to hear what the person is expressing

- Responding in ways that are helpful *when help is called for* (which it usually isn't)

Let's look at how we put these ideas into practice.

Skill 1: Focus

Focusing our attention has a lot to do with what we *aren't* thinking about. You need to empty your mind of concerns and worries, letting go of your own eagerness to be heard. Break the habit of looking for a pause where you can jump back in. Slow your breathing down, noticing your breath going in and out. Relax, letting go consciously of the need to speak. If there are empty places inside you, remind yourself, "Listening well often fills the emptiness better than talking."

When there is a pause, wait to see if the person will continue. Some of the most important feelings and thoughts are expressed after a few moments of quiet, so it's important to leave spaces. If you sense that the person isn't going to continue, ask a question to draw him or her out further.

One of the goals, then, is to *slow down the exchange of roles*. In a typical conversation, people switch speaking roles more than once per minute, with each person switching the subject back to "me." This pace leads both people to feel unheard.

Train yourself instead to focus on the other person for several minutes, carefully digesting what they're saying. You're on a voyage through the other person's inner world, getting familiar with the amazing and varied landscape inside them.

Think of yourself as building a muscle or learning a spiritual discipline. See if you can listen to a friend or a relative for five minutes without switching the subject to yourself, then try for ten, then fifteen. You'll develop the ability to give focused attention to another person for longer and longer stretches. Daily exercise and stress reduction techniques can also help you build your attention span.

Skill 2: Give the Speaker Your Eyes

Develop the habit of keeping your eyes on the other person's eyes while he or she talks. The person speaking can gaze at the sky the whole time if that helps them get their thoughts and feelings out; but the listener should look them right in the eye. *The single greatest factor in whether a person feels listened to is having the other person's eyes solidly on them and always available.*

Your eyes don't need to bore holes in the other person; in fact, the speaker can get distracted if you stare intensely. Relax your face and eyes, gazing at the person with calm, caring attention.

Skill 3: Do Less

Listening is an arena where the saying "less is more" aptly applies. Avoid saying, "Uh-huh, uh-huh," or using any similar verbal tic. Don't fidget with your phone, don't get up and down a lot. Try to stop everything and just listen. An *occasional* well-spaced, "I see what you mean," or "Wow!" is all it takes to show that you are hearing; your nods and facial expressions also communicate your caring. Beyond that, try to keep quiet and still. Your eyes, and the questions you ask, will show the other person that you're taking it all in.

Skill 4: Don't Fix It

When we're trying to listen, most of us have distracting thoughts such as:

- "What can I say to help the person feel better?"

- "I need to come up with some suggestions."

- "Maybe I should share about a similar thing that happened to me."

- "I wish I could think of some wisdom to offer. Maybe I should at least say, 'It is what it is,' or some other popular phrase."

Wouldn't it be lovely to escape this pressure? You can. Believe it or not, advice or suggestions rarely help. Keep responses of this kind to less than 5%; make the lion's share of what you offer be support, validation, and thoughtful questions. These gifts will help the person far more than problem-solving will.

When you break the fix-it habit, you'll relax and start to enjoy listening to people rather than finding it burdensome. As a result, people speaking to you will feel your presence more and benefit from it. *Notice this irony: the less we try to help, the more we help.*

Helping isn't even the main goal. What matters most is to *connect*; that's the deepest human desire, whether we're talking or listening at the moment.

Skill 5: Give Support and Validation

Our goal as listeners is not just to be supportive, but to make the other person feel our support.

Let's look at three common ways of responding that we want to avoid:

1. Saying, "I know what you mean, because there was a time when…" and launching into talking about ourselves

Break the habit of responding with a story of your own. If you have a story to share that you think might help (or that you're just plain dying to tell), keep it short or, even better, say, "I've been through something similar myself but let's come back to that later." Be especially cautious not to outdo what the other person shared (by saying, for example, "You think that's bad, listen to this…"), which is invalidating.

2. Acting so upset about what the other person is going through that we seem sadder or angrier than they are

Believe it or not, acting too sympathetic gets in the way. There's an art to letting the person know that you're upset by what they're going through without letting your own feelings take the foreground. Plus you don't want the speaker to worry that they're burdening you.

I've been asked a number of times, "Is it okay if I start crying from what the other person just told me?" Absolutely; just keep your crying quiet so as not to steal the spotlight, and keep your eyes on the other person. As long as they don't lose your attention, it will feel good to them that you were moved by what they shared. If they express concern, just say, "I'm totally fine, please keep going with what you were saying."

3. Saying, "I know exactly how you feel"

It isn't possible to know exactly what someone feels. You can imagine what you would feel in their circumstances, but that's not the same. The speaker wants to feel that you get what their experience is like for *them*. And you get there by asking questions. Ironically, the more you accept that you can't perfectly understand the other person's feelings, the better able you'll be to grasp their experience.

When the person is describing an extreme experience, you can go the opposite way and express that you *can't* imagine what it was like for them. This response helps the person feel that you get the severity of what happened.

Some Great Supportive Responses

Express understanding and offer validation, as in:

- "That sounds hard."

- "Does that make you angry?"

- "Of course you would feel upset."

- "That must be really sad."

Point out injustices. Some examples include:

- "Your boss shouldn't have treated you that way."

- "You haven't done anything to deserve that from her."

- "I don't care what his excuses are, that doesn't make it okay."

- "It sounds like you got a racist response from that person."

Mention strengths, including things that the speaker has done well. These could include:

- "Well, at least you said some things that really needed saying."

- "You should be proud of how well you stood up for yourself."

- "She's saying you dropped the ball, but I think you've actually been doing a great job."

It's important to be honest, though; don't encourage people to avoid looking at mistakes they've made. Instead, look for genuinely positive aspects to point out.

Draw upon your own feelings toward the person, as in:

- "I'm happy to be with you no matter how you're feeling, don't worry about being downhearted." (because people often think that they're a burden when they're having a hard time)

- "I think you're such a good person, I think very highly of you." (if they're telling you about someone who put them down)

- "I find you very smart." (if they're questioning their own intelligence; but remember to follow a comment like this with, "But I get it that you're not feeling smart right now" — always let people feel what they're feeling)

Allow silence. The person speaking will be better able to digest your support if you leave pauses and generally slow everything down. Periods of quiet will also help them feel their feelings. Say just enough so that the person can tell you're still there.

Show your support physically. Give the person a hug, touch their forearm, put a hand on their shoulder, squeeze their hand. The most important support is communicated without words.

However, when you put a supportive hand on a person who is expressing distress, keep your hand *still*. Patting, rubbing, or stroking distracts them from their feelings, and can make them feel like you want them to stop crying. A still hand communicates the message, "Go ahead and feel what you're feeling. I'll be here with you through it."

Pay careful attention to make sure that physical contact is welcome. If the person shows any sign of discomfort or pulls away at all, don't continue the touch. (And if the person is sharing about an experience of invasion — for example, telling you that they were sexually mistreated — don't give supportive touch without first asking if that's okay.)

Offer concrete assistance when it fits. Sometimes being supportive means looking after their children for half an hour so they can go for a walk to decompress, accompanying them into a difficult situation, or making them food when they've been too upset to eat well.

Give validation. The basic principles of validation involve letting the person know that:

- you understand what they're feeling.

- you think their feelings make sense and are natural responses given what they're dealing with.

- you don't think they're overreacting.

- you believe them.

These don't always need to be said in words; you can get those points across through warm facial expression and caring questions.

As always, be genuine; it's best not to validate feelings that seem way off to you. But don't shoot down what the person said; invalidation can feel crushing to someone in a painful place. Validate whatever parts you feel you can, and leave the rest aside. (If there are things you really need to challenge the person about, do it later, not while they're opening up to you for support.)

Skill 6: Ask Questions, Questions, and More Questions

The art of asking questions is fading, and needs to be brought vigorously back to life. Questions connect us. Through our questions, we communicate to people that we're interested in their lives and their feelings. Questions invite people to tell about themselves; most people won't open up until they're sure you want to hear it. And questions help people think about their lives from a new angle. If you're not asking questions much, you're missing the opportunity to really connect.

Here's what to ask:

Questions that encourage the person to say more. Many people worry that they're burdening or boring you if they talk at length. So ask questions such as:

- "What happened before that? What happened after?"

- "Can you explain more about what was going on?"

- "What was that like for you?"

- "What was going on in your mind while this was occurring?"

- "Tell me more about that."

This last one may sound awkward to you at first—as though you're interviewing the person—but it soon comes to feel natural and you'll love the places it leads. It's always there when you can't think of what to ask.

Questions to go deeper. Let the person know you're reflecting on what he or she is saying, by asking things like:

- "Why do you think she did that?" (when the person is mystified by someone else's actions)

- "Has she raised these questions in the past, or is this brand new?" (to a person describing a difficult interaction with a supervisor)

- "Is this triggering anything from your past?" (when the person expresses not understanding his or her own reaction to an event)

- "Do you think there's an underlying issue?" (when the person reports a tense argument with a partner over a small matter, for example)

At the same time, avoid expressing judgment through the questions you ask. We need to believe what people tell us about their lives.

Questions that make connections, such as:

- "Is this similar to what happened that other time?"

- "Is this making it hard for you to get your work done?"

- "Does this affect your thoughts of having a child?"

- "Didn't he just do exactly what you had asked him not to do?"

Questions that show you remember what he or she has told you in the past. This is a big one. Questions that refer to what you already know about the person demonstrate that you have been thinking about them. To be a good asker of questions, work on strengthening your *memory* of what you hear, by: 1) increasing your focus when someone is speaking, and 2) consciously going over a conversation in your mind for a few minutes when it's over.

Tracking Themes

There's a final key to asking good questions: *Keeping mental track of the themes in the speaker's life.* If we could all learn to do this for the people we care about, the impact would be tremendous.

Say you and your friend Kai decide to meet for a morning walk in the park. While you're getting ready to leave your apartment, you think about the threads that make up the fabric of Kai's life. He's in a long-term relationship with

Megan and you remember some of their recurring issues, such as Kai's wish that they'd spend more time outdoors and Megan's eagerness to start a family. Next you think about Kai's work, which he likes, but he's concerned the company may not stay afloat. That reminds you of another uncertainty, which is that his mother is getting old but wants to remain in her own home, and Kai needs more help with her than he's getting from his siblings.

As you walk with Kai, keep these themes in the back of your mind, looking for natural opportunities to point the conversation towards them. Your efforts in this direction will lead Kai to feel that you grasp, and care about, what is important to him. Keeping track of a person's life themes also helps you avoid the "I can't think of what to ask" problem.

When the Person Does Want Advice

Sometimes a person directly asks, "What do you think I should do?" First, remember that you're never obligated to give advice. You may have no idea what would help, or you may feel that the person needs to trust his or her own judgment. (Or you might be afraid of being blamed later for giving "bad" advice, as when dealing with a moody boss or a not-so-healthy relative.)

If you feel open to sharing your suggestions:

- Don't hesitate to ask questions first to learn more about the situation.

- If you're sharing what has worked for you—which can definitely be helpful—you might also remind the person that what works for one person isn't always good for another.

- Avoid a tone that sounds too sure that you know what is best; pressuring people is a mistake, for many reasons.

- Share any resources you think of (people for them to consult, books or websites to read, agencies to call) to increase the support they can draw upon.

- Try to come up with suggestions that help the person develop his or her own problem-solving skills, rather than solving the problem yourself. For example, you can lay out the pros and cons that you see in each choice, rather than telling them which path to take.

Say, for example, that a friend of yours asks for advice about her relationship, and you think her boyfriend is mistreating her. Instead of saying, "He's bad news, you need to break up with him," you do better to say, "I'll lend you a book that helps women sort out whether their partner's behavior is abusive or not." In this way you equip her to make her own decisions, helping her regain control of her life.

Look for ways to shift the discussion back toward the person's own thinking. Ask them what they've tried, what has worked and not worked in the past, what outcome they're looking for. One of the best questions is, "What do *you* think you should do?"

Finally, don't swamp a person with advice. Give one or two ideas for now. Any of us, when struggling with life's greater challenges, can take in only a little information at a time.

When Someone is in Severe Distress

If we're listening to a person who is super upset, we can start to feel that we're in over our heads. The first question to assess is whether the person is at risk to harm themselves or someone else. If so, don't handle it alone; reach out to a friend or a hotline, and if the risk is immediate, call 911 (in the U.S.). In the mean time, keep your voice gentle and your body posture non-threatening, so you don't escalate the person further. Avoid telling them repeatedly to calm down, as this can easily get them *more* agitated.

Apart from emergency situations, don't try to calm people down. Let them have their feelings. Try not to get stressed by their stress; keep breathing and remind yourself that they're okay. You don't have to fix anything. Just focus on being present. If other people around you notice and appear stressed, try to move away from them.

What a deeply upset person most needs from you, besides your love and attention, is your solidity; strive to look and sound strong even if you feel shaky inside. Validate their feelings and show that you understand. You can gently offer reassurance, such as telling them that you think they'll be okay; but if they react negatively to reassurance, let that go and focus on supporting them in other ways.

If you need to leave, make a clear plan with the person for the hours ahead. Is anyone else available to support them today? Are there any tough situations coming up that they must deal with? Do they feel okay about your leaving? Consider making specific agreements, such as, "Call me in two hours and let me know how it went," or, "Can you promise me you won't go back home until you've spoken to your counselor?"

If you think the person may go over the edge if you leave, stay there until someone else can take over. In general, we need to learn to be more comfortable with people who are deeply upset; modern culture keeps people on too tight of a leash emotionally. But we also want to make sure to be safe.

We tend to get especially concerned when someone is crying, but these are generally the people we need to worry about the *least*; as I explain in Chapter 8, all you need to do is provide love and support while allowing them to cry for as long as they need to.

Key Points to Remember:

- Talking doesn't help our healing much unless we have a strong connection with the person we're talking to. And the way to forge that connection is to *listen*.

- Even the best listeners have volumes to learn about how to connect through listening and how to support another person.

- Learn to ask people lots of questions and listen carefully to their answers.

Chapter Five

What's Right With You

The Peak Living Network approach can't fix you. Why not? Because there's nothing wrong with you. You don't need a repair job, you need to *heal*.

Suppose you skidded in sand on your bicycle, fell onto pavement, and broke your arm. Now your arm doesn't work, plus it's in terrible pain. There's clearly a problem. But is anything fundamentally *wrong* with your arm? No, it's just cracked. *All we need to do is create the proper context for your arm to heal*. We need to line up the bones correctly, protect your vulnerable arm for several weeks, and feed your body nutrients that support bone growth. Beyond these steps, we need to allow natural processes to work; more intervention would just get in the way.

What would happen if, instead, we took the view that there was something truly wrong with your arm? First, you would feel downhearted and, as studies have shown, that would slow your healing. Next you would try surgery, which would make your recovery take way longer, might lead to unwanted effects, and would throw off other aspects of your health.

It works much better to say, "My arm is totally sound. I just need to make sure the bone has what it needs for healing." An additional great step is to tell yourself, "I want to get back to riding my bike and playing my guitar, so I'm going to handle my healing in a way that will allow my arm to do those things again."

This is the same mindset I want you to bring to your *emotional* recovery. There's nothing wrong with you; your spirit just needs you to create the right context for it to heal. Meanwhile, set your sights not on what you want to *change* or *fix*, but instead on what you *want to be able to do*.

Here are examples of thinking to steer away from:

- "I need to stop being so neurotic."

- "I need to conquer my fears."

- "I want to be less suspicious of people."

- "I've got to cut down on eating junk food."

Aim yourself instead toward goals that sound more like:

- "I want to spend more time doing what matters most to me."

- "I want to take more risks."

- "I want to have closer relationships."

- "I want to have lots of energy and feel good after I eat."

We heal better when we focus on what *capacities* we want to develop, rather than what "bad" aspects of ourselves we want to get rid of.

Looking at What You've Done Well So Far

You've already accomplished far more than you realize. Let's go on a tour of what you've done.

1. You Have Survived

Survival has required vast strength, courage, and ingenuity from you. It has demanded that you value yourself when the world around you was failing to do so. By getting to where you are today—alive and functioning—you've proven that:

- you have mind-boggling strength.

- you have a fierce desire to live.

- you are capable of fighting back (even if largely in hidden ways).

- you are creative in finding ways to get through it all.

- you are capable of focusing on positive aspects of life in the midst of great pain.

Even if at the present moment you feel weak and helpless, shredded by life—and the truth is that we all have those times—the reality is that you're a person of stunning capability in the middle of firestorms; otherwise you wouldn't be here.

Start telling yourself what a proud survivor you are, what a miracle it is that you're still walking and talking. As a dear co-counselor of mine named Charles once said to me, "At those dark times in life, you were doing amazing if you could put one foot in front of the other."

Those of you whose memories of darkness are completely blocked may feel that I'm exaggerating, that nothing that bad ever happened to you. It isn't my mission to convince you otherwise. I will continue to see you as a miracle whether you see yourself that way or not.

Survival Strategies Were Smart at the Time
We carry shame and self-criticism about the behavior pat-

terns we carry. But in truth even the patterns that are the most unhealthy now served to keep us alive at the time we developed them. They were not a mistake back then.

This is why programs that reward good behaviors in children and "get tough" with bad behaviors work only briefly, if at all. If you don't address a child's circumstances, including the need for healing, he or she is going to continue to need those "dysfunctional" behaviors.[1]

In reflecting on your own patterns, ask yourself:

"When I first started doing this, how did it help me get through?"

"What was smart about developing this pattern *considering what the alternatives were for me at the time*?"

Let's say that at a certain point in childhood you started to knock down other kids' block towers, pour glue on their art projects, and drop a kickball onto their animal villages. What was this accomplishing?

- You were creating a huge stir that made you feel powerful, relieving some of the powerlessness you were feeling about big distresses in your life.

- You were getting yourself into huge painful trouble, and that pain drove out the far worse pain of other things you were experiencing. (Certain kinds of pain are preferable to others; for example, people sometimes hurt themselves physically to drive away intolerable emotional pain.)

- You got to be the focus of attention, which you desperately needed.

[1] See *The Child Survivor* by Dr. Joyanna Silberg

- Your actions gave you a channel for your rage about other issues.

A common response to these points is, "Well, but I could have chosen much healthier ways to cope."

No! If you could have, you would have. Kids only go in these problematic directions *when they find all the better paths closed*. One way to decrease your self-blame is to examine the question, "What made it impossible for me to get what I needed in some other way?"

I get it that these patterns are working against you in the present and need to go. But taking pride in the creative, courageous way you developed these survival strategies will actually help you get past them.

Like all of us, you've come through nasty sicknesses, the losses of loved ones, injustices, and dark despairing times. Think of the courage and toughness it has taken you to get through. You stood up and dusted yourself off time after time when life knocked you down. Take pride in the fact that you're on your feet.

2. You Have Loved People

Love is the most beautiful force in the human world. You have participated in that blessing and furthered it. Each time that you've loved someone, that was a triumph.

Loving people is risky. They can ignore you, reject you, or even ridicule you for showing love. They can turn against you, or stop needing you. They can pass away or move away. They can disillusion you. You have chosen to love people in the face of these risks, and your love has been a gift to them—whether they acknowledged it or not—and to the world.

Think about the people you have most loved, whether briefly or for many years, the ones who are still in your life today and the ones not. Try to remember *all* of them. All of that love—all of that beauty that you have sent out into the world—*matters*. You have proven your soulful capacity to give love.

Remember also the love you've felt and shown to animals and other living things.

Take additional pride in anyone you loved in these circumstances:

- after being taught not to love them

- when other people were undervaluing them

- even though they couldn't give much in return

- when loving them was scary or risky

- despite the fact that they weren't healthy people (and even if eventually you had to avoid them for your own well-being)

You've still got a beating heart, and there's so much love that you're still going to give.

3. You Have Fought For What Is Right

You may not feel like a crusader, but in reality you've stood up for justice at many points dating back to when you were very young. You have a personal history of resisting mistreatment toward yourself and other people, however forgotten it may be.

Consider how young children react to seeing another child or an animal get seriously hurt; they wail in distress at seeing any being suffer. If the hurt they're witnessing involves any aspect of injustice they become even more up-set; children are quite preoccupied with fairness.

For children to stop caring about others in this way it has to be beaten out of them. When you see a callous, self-ish child, you're seeing someone who has been broken by experiencing or witnessing chronic severe mistreatment. (He or she may not fit your idea of what a broken-hearted child would look like, though; we often survive trauma by adopting a mask that is the polar opposite of how down-trodden we feel.)

In short, kids become uncaring by having their caring trampled upon, selfish by having their generosity devastat-ed, bigoted by being insulted for valuing people they were told not to value.

Children become both saddened and resistant when they are first taught racist or sexist attitudes, and they clearly *don't want to go along with it*. They hate divisions. Children have to have bad attitudes drilled into them for a long time before they give in. *You have a personal history of this reluc-tance to participate in injustice.*

Invisible Resistance Matters

Children face powerful intimidation, ranging from with-ering sarcasm to outright physical harm, for saying what they really think. The result is that much of a child's bit-terness about injustice is kept inside, unspoken and unex-pressed. Recognizing the ways in which you silently held on to your objections to mistreatment, toward you or to-ward others, is part of collecting your history of resistance to wrongs. I can remember how bitter I felt as a child about how adults treated children, *but I hardly ever told anyone, not even other kids.* Keeping your true beliefs alive inside is a form of not giving up.

4. You've Been Smart

Despite how bad you may feel about the mistakes you've made over the years—we've all done things we regret—the reality is that you've proven your intelligence many times. I'm going to ask you to start examining that history.

A key reason why people feel stupid is *school*. At one time or another school makes everyone feel that they aren't very bright. For lots of kids it hammers them with that message day after day, for example:

- students who are hungry or exhausted because of too little food or too much pain at home so they can't listen well

- students who can't bear to sit still

- students who are not very strong at "book smarts"— there are eight or more known styles of intelligence, but school recognizes and rewards only one or two

- students who misbehave at school, which can be happening for all kinds of reasons

- students who don't do well on tests or who are highly anxious

Moreover, school actually encourages students to compare themselves to others (a vast mistake) through the giving of grades and the emphasis on winning the teacher's approval.

And, of course, school is just one challenge. In Chapter 2 I discussed several ways in which we've been given false messages about our intelligence.

A key beginning piece to your healing work, then, is to take an inventory of the ways your thinking has been good over the years. Consider the following questions:

- What decisions or choices have you made that have had positive outcomes? *(Many aspects of intelligence)*

- What were times when you figured out that a bad way someone treated you (or someone else) was not right? *(Justice intelligence)*

- What creative arts have you engaged in (even in secret), such as drawing, music, acting, dance? *(Creative intelligence)*

- What have you built? What have you repaired? *(Creative intelligence, mechanical intelligence)*

- What problems have you solved? (Though you may draw a blank at first, I can promise you that you've solved countless problems in your life and probably do so every day.) *(Problem-solving intelligence)*

- What are ways you have used your body well, such as in athletics, dance, or precise handwork? *(Physical intelligence)*

- What insights into complex human emotions have you brought to your relationships or shared with people to help them with struggles? What are ways you have been understanding of other people's experiences? *(Emotional intelligence)*

- What are ways you have worked well with others, whether in pairs or in groups? *(Cooperative intelligence)*

- What are ways in which you have done well in school or shown "book smarts"? *(Linear intelligence and logic)*

I want you to throw out the entire idea that some people are smarter than others. When we look across the full range of intelligence styles, the question of who is smarter becomes meaningless. Everyone has skills and insights to bring to the table. We need to learn to draw out the strengths from each person's intelligence, and from our own. We desperately need what everyone has to offer.

5. You've Been Brave

Just as there aren't smart and not-smart people, there aren't brave and not-brave people. Some people's courage is more outwardly obvious, but everyone has taken impressive risks and has a history of courage. If we knew the full story of what people had been up against in their lives, we'd be stunned by their bravery.

Courage is often misunderstood as meaning "to be unafraid." But if you feel no fear, carrying out an act doesn't require courage, does it? Additionally, much of the behavior that gets called "brave" is actually foolhardy; when people feel no fear, they endanger themselves and others. Courage is shown when you take a positive action *despite how scary it is.*

I've had people confide in me that they find every day pretty scary; but through willpower, faith, and great courage they manage to push through over and over again.

Let me give examples of brave actions that you might not think of that way:

- leaving a relationship that was not healthful for you, despite having to sacrifice comfort and security in order to leave

- telling lies to adults when you were a kid in order to keep yourself or other people out of trouble

- running from a conflict where you were going to get hurt, despite knowing that other people would ridicule you for fleeing (yup, that's *courageous*—and smart)

- moving out of the home you grew up in, striking out on your own

- standing up to a boss about workplace issues, trying to persuade other employees to take a stand, or quitting a job because you deserve better

- living in ways that are not socially acceptable or weren't at the time (dressing differently, being lesbian or gay, being yourself even though other people considered you odd, taking unpopular political stands)

- endless other examples of tackling situations that were scary for you—*whether other people would find them scary or not*—and carrying on despite the fear

Take an inventory of the courageous risks you've taken.

6. You've Contributed To the World

One of the deepest human desires is to give significantly to the people we love and to our wider community, and to have what we offer be noticed and appreciated. Contemplate the sense of satisfaction felt by members of a tribe as they cure and store food to keep the collective fed and warm through the cold winter. Each person knows, "I was part of this accomplishment, and look what it has done for us all."

This desire is difficult to satisfy in the modern world where our work is so often controlled by people (and computers) far away from us or who have no real interest in the well-being of our community. *Feeling blocked regarding our ability to contribute is one of the most powerful, but least recognized, causes of modern unhappiness.*

I've already asked you to think about the love you've poured into the world and about the ways you have stood for what is right. Now reflect on your contributions in these other areas:

Helping to build connections and resolve conflicts or separations

Think about times, with children or adults, when you've helped people understand each other, encouraged people to be more patient with each other, or assisted people to communicate. Perhaps you've helped people get back in touch who had lost contact, helped people who had become alienated work out a reconnection, or helped an individual find a group that was a good fit to join.

Being there for people in times of need or for significant life events

Remember times when you've been present for health crises or after accidents, showing up for people when big challenges or losses struck. Think also about the importance of your presence at weddings, funerals, births, graduations, and rites of passage (such as first communions or bar mitzvahs). It matters that you were there; you gave to the world by joining those crucial human gatherings.

Your unpaid work

The most powerful examples in this category are the raising of children and caregiving for the old or chronically ill. Parents pour endless energy, love, and problem-solving into giving the world one of its greatest desires, which is to see the next generation growing. Unpaid work also includes volunteering for charitable or community-development work, doing labor to help friends or relatives, and more. Millions of people around the globe work 40 and 50 and 60 hours a week with no compensation while handling some of the world's most important responsibilities.

Your paid work

One of the outrages of modern life is that so many people lose their human right to be engaged in labor that is good for the world. I hope that you're among the fortunate people who've been able to earn a living making a visible contribution. Perhaps you've been able to work in such fields as food production or preparation, child care, education, social services, or other line of work that allows you to go to sleep at night knowing that the world is benefiting from your labor.

Working for justice and the environment

Activism is valuable work (a point ignored by passing bullies who yell, "Why don't you get a job?" at people in demonstrations). If you've ever stood at a vigil, joined a march, or attended meetings of people working for a cause, you've pitched in. Activism also includes: working on a union at your workplace; being part of a strike, slow down, or "sick out" at work; confronting corporate or elected officials; filing a legal challenge in the public interest; and myriad other forms of resistance. The world urgently needs people who keep fighting for the belief that life could be different.

Creating

Painters, sculptors, ceramicists, actors, musicians, dancers—we owe so much to all these creative people for enhancing the beauty of our world, for showing us truths and insights about ourselves, and for contributing to the fight for a better world. In the words of the P.O.S. song: "This is for all the artists who know their work is just a drop in the ocean but do it anyway, hoping."[2]

In the Peak Living Network we look for the strength in ourselves and in others. As we listen to each other's stories, we turn our ears to pick up the triumphs, the courage, and the gifts of the heart, *and we strive to reflect those back to each other*. We develop habits of saying, "Wow, that was such a smart thing you did," or "I'm impressed by how brave you were," or "I'm amazed that you were able to endure all that and still live as well as you do." These truths about each other's accomplishments and strengths are a beautiful reality to hold up to the light.

We learn to focus on what we've done well, our capabilities, how much love is in our hearts, and how we can keep opening up the path ahead of us. We work to notice, about ourselves and each other:

- what great people we are

- what dark places we have fought our way through and out of

- what noble risks we've taken to seek freedom, or so that loved ones could be well

- how smart we've been, often in ways that no one noticed

This awareness is a pillar in the structure of a network that heals joyfully.

[2] From "Music for Shoplifting" by P.O.S. from the CD Ipecac Neat, Rhymesayers Entertainment

Move Forward As If These Things Were True About You

Start now acting on the assumption that you are a smart, appealing, competent person. Don't wait until you can believe in your strengths—that might be quite far in the future. Act on the basis of what your deepest wisdom is telling you, not on the basis of those negative voices in your head. Each day ask yourself:

"How would I handle things if I believed in my value?"

"What would I do if I weren't afraid?"

"What choices would I make if I believed that other people wanted to see me do well?"

Then follow where your answers take you.

Key Points to Remember:

- Healing builds from strength. Begin by taking an inventory of what you've done well.

- You have a personal history of courage, creativity, generosity, and resistance to injustice.

- We all have such a history. Let's remind each other of that fact frequently.

Chapter Six

Telling the Truth

Imagine what it would be like to have a few people who *really* knew your story. They knew the ups and downs of your life, the triumphs and the tragedies, the times of excitement and euphoria, the times of terrifying, impenetrable darkness. And they not only knew the events, but they grasped what all these hills, fields and valleys had actually *meant* to you.

Human injury, when left unhealed, becomes locked in place. One of the locks in the system is that our wounds become increasingly difficult to talk about, write about, make art about, or scream about because:

- we start to forget what has happened.

- we start to minimize it, deciding it wasn't that big a deal.

- we get told by other people (sometimes the very people who've harmed us) that we're exaggerating our injuries or that the hurtful events never took place.

- we get tired of the responses we receive when we open up about the truth (from people who are too distracted to listen and don't ask questions, or who give us philosophical responses instead of absorbing what we're saying, or who blame us for what happened).

- we become afraid of burdening people, or afraid they'll feel sorry for us.

- we lose hope that expressing our experiences will make any difference.

The healing power of sharing our stories is misunderstood. But, interestingly, the limitations of sharing them are not understood either. Consider the following key points:

1) Expressing the truth, both good and bad, of what your life has been like is profoundly important to healing. The secrets never revealed, the history lost to memory, and the feelings never described need to be unearthed and shared.

2) At the same time, *expressing our histories and our pain won't do enough by itself.* You might say that you can't build a reliable house without a good foundation, but you also can't live on just a foundation.

Telling the truth is an indispensable step, but it's just the first one.

Telling the truth is often taken to mean, "opening up about how horrible it has been." But it's equally important to bring to light the people we've wholeheartedly loved, the places that have been dear to us, the moments we've cherished, the acts we've taken pride in. People speak of the need to explore our "dark side," but rarely mention the importance of reconnecting with our past joys and triumphs. Those unexpressed moments of joy are holding back our healing *just as much* as unexpressed pain.

Begin Now

I want you to start your exploration of truth-telling by writing something unlike anything you've written before: Write the story of your life in about 1500 words. Let's say not fewer than 1250 nor more than 1750. That's about five pages of double-spaced text. The reason to set an upper limit is so that you zero in on what has mattered the most to you.

I'm not asking you to write a chronology of events. Instead, see if you can describe what the events in your life have *meant* to you, what their significance has been. You might address, for example:

- What would I most want a loved one to understand about what things have been like for me?

- What do I most need to say, including pieces that I have not yet expressed?

- What have I most cared about? What pieces of my caring (toward people, toward beliefs, toward animals or places) have I not yet allowed to fully show?

- What are my deepest satisfactions? And what are my deepest longings? When has my heart most soared? When did it most break?

Write this piece under the assumption that you will *show it to no one*. If you decide later to share part or all of it that's fine; but don't hold anything back in this first version out of concern for how it might sound, or because it might hurt someone or make them angry. You can omit those pieces later *if* you decide to share what you wrote.

Next...

Do you have other avenues through which you could express your experience, such as artwork, dancing, writing poems, acting, or singing? (Even if you do these things only for yourself, it still counts.) Over the next few weeks, look for pieces of your history that you could allow to take shape through one of these forms, drawing upon the questions listed above.

If you don't feel able to try any of these forms, continue with your writing, but now forget the word limit and turn yourself loose.

Bringing Truth to Conversations

Consider how telling the whole truth can enter into your time with friends or relatives. As you're sharing life's events and dramas, ask yourself:

"What might I say now that I haven't said before?"

"What aspect of what I feel could I reveal newly?"

"How could I bring a different level of sincerity to our time together?"

"How could I lead this interaction in a direction where we'd open up more with each other?"

You can deepen the exchange with what you ask, not just with what you say. An unexpected prompt, such as, "What was that time really like for you?" or "Tell me more about that period in your life," can surprise a person into opening up.

Notice when your conversation goes over ground that you've already traveled many times, and take that as a signal that it's time for creativity. Experiment, seeing how you might send yourself or your loved one in a new or deeper direction.

I'm not advising you to open up with people who have hurt you in the past. We all know individuals who've proven that they can't reliably hold our hearts in their hands; with them we need to open up *less*, not more. But there are other people in our lives with whom our exchanges have settled into predictability out of habit or comfort or fear. Now it's time to shake things up by daring to tell the truth and inviting others to do the same.

People Who Never Hold Their Stories Back

There are people who seem to have no trouble broadcasting their feelings, dramas, and wounds. In fact, some folks pour their thoughts and pain out to like a geyser to anyone who will listen, seeming unable to stop themselves. If your tendency is in this direction, you may actually need to tell the truth less. Work instead on developing stronger boundaries, making careful choices about who sees into your inner world. Overexposure is not helpful to healing.

Even people who open up too much, though, have important pieces of their experience that they have never shared. So the question still applies, "What parts of me is it time to allow someone to see?"

———————

In Part Two of this book, I explain how to propel yourself toward healing through:

- working in healing partnerships.

- creating the right rhythm between healing and action.

- confronting injustice.

- using your inherent emotional release processes, your body's natural plan for emotional recovery.

These are the keys to lasting and transformative emotional healing. But they depend on your commitment, growing over time, to express the truth of your history and experience. In the Peak Living Network, we want to know what things have been like for you. Become a truth-teller, and become someone who invites others—not by pressuring or lecturing, but by opening doors—to join you in doing so.

Key Points to Remember:

- Seek out people whom you trust enough to reveal more and more of the realities of your inner world, both past and present.

- Get brave about letting more of yourself show—while still using good judgment about which people are safe to expose your feelings to.

- The more we know about each other, the more love, support, and healing we can share.

Chapter Seven

Building a Support System

I want to see you floating contentedly in a sea of love. That's how human beings are designed to live, that's when we fully shine.

In the modern world it has come to be seen as normal to spend our lives battling against loneliness and disconnection, taking on challenges alone, and having only occasional moments when we feel close to someone. But we weren't meant to live that way.

I'm going to ask you to make the strengthening and nurturing of your support system one of your central focuses for at least the next year. Even after that, it will require ongoing care and attention. If you already feel well-supported—and I'm happy if you're one of the lucky ones—I encourage you to make your support network even better.

What Does Good Support Look Like?

We've looked at various aspects of what makes effective and soothing support, which I'll summarize here:

- people who listen well; their attention is focused, their eye contact is good, they don't feel the need to quickly switch the subject back to themselves

- people who are on your side the great majority of the time, not criticizing you or questioning your decisions for no real reason; and when they do raise concerns, it's rooted in caring about you

- people who remember what you've shared with them in the past

- people who come through for you at the most important times; they're on the scene when you have a great success, when you're badly ill, or when you have a painful loss

- people who do their share of the reaching out, who make you feel that you matter and are important to them

- people who accept support and assistance from you

- people who are physically affectionate in ways that are appropriate and that feel good to you

- people who respond well when you're upset, including when you're crying

As you get better and better at listening to others, I hope you'll also come to expect that quality of listening in return. Notice who listens really well and who doesn't, and allow that to influence your choices about which people are a priority in your life.

When I say that people should be behind you most of the time, that means steer away from people who:

- keep telling you what they think you should do differently.

- keep telling you that you have the wrong outlook (such as that you "shouldn't let things bother you").

- often put you on the defensive, so that you leave the interaction with the person feeling that you had to prove something or convince them of something.

Loved ones don't owe you blind loyalty. There certainly can be times when they need to say things that are hard for you to hear, but it isn't good for you if they take these steps from habits of being critical or oppositional. You can feel the difference.

Support needs to be *mutual*. It doesn't have to even out every day, but over time each relationship should feel balanced. If you're putting your own needs aside while a loved one goes through a difficult period, you should be able to expect the same in return when you're the one who hits a rough spot.

What this means in practical terms is that you need to reduce the time you spend with people whose lives are a non-stop flow of drama. And, similarly, if you have habits of coming to your friends with a crisis-of-the-week, work to break out of that cycle.

Occasionally people are out of balance in the opposite direction; they give lots of support to others but open up little about their own highs and lows and don't accept caretaking. This, too, is a problem. Seek people who accept assistance as well as provide it, who are willing to take a turn in the vulnerable position.

Touch

Physical affection is an indispensable aspect of emotional support. You need your loved ones to be able to put a hand on your arm, throw an arm around your shoulder, and come through with a tight, lasting hug when you need one. They need to be capable of holding you when you're crying.

I recognize that this can be hard to find, depending on your social world or culture. But touch is one of the most powerful communicators of caring and safety, and deep healing depends on physical contact (though not necessarily right away, as I discuss later).

Support and Healing Are a Feedback Loop

It's easy to tell yourself—at least on a bad day—"I can't build close relationships right now, I'm too depressed, there's no one around here that I like very much, I'm too busy trying to pay the rent." Most of us get caught in this trap at some point, needing more support in order to heal but simultaneously needing to heal before feeling strong enough to reach out. What's the solution?

One answer lies in scaling our goals back (just for now). Little steps toward human connection give us strength to move forward in working through our distresses. In turn, that small emotional improvement gives us the courage to take another risk toward finding closeness. Back and forth we go, our support system feeding our healing and our healing feeding our ability to cultivate support.

It's important, then, not to wait for it to be the "right time," when you feel ready to do something big. Go ahead today and take an initiative of some kind, even one that the voices in your head label "meaningless." It won't be. Make a call, send a text, spend a little extra time talking to the cashier at the supermarket, connect any way you can.

Finding People Takes Work

We live in a historical period when the social forces pulling us away from each other are greater than the forces pulling us together. Modern society is highly hierarchical, and hierarchy leads to separation, loneliness, and the dismantling of communities. Loneliness is not a natural fact of life, nor is it your private battle; it's a challenge for almost everyone nowadays.

And isolation can be overcome if you make conscious, determined effort. It is a battle, but *it's a battle that can be won.*

Let's look at some avenues to pursue:

1. Strategies for meeting new people:

Almost all of us feel the need to broaden our social horizons, to make new friends as old friendships fade or rupture, and to just plain have more people in our lives. Some great ways to reach out include:

Attend a faith community (church, temple, mosque, etc.)

If no faith community fits you so far, try visiting a different one every week (yes, people really do this) until you find one you like. If you're an atheist, you might check out a spiritual community where believing in God isn't required such as Unitarian Universalist.

Pursue your interests

It's often said that the best way to meet people that you're compatible with is to pursue the activities you most enjoy. Here's a random list to stimulate possibilities in your mind: quilting, volleyball, hiking, bird watching, volunteering, social justice activism, book clubs, biking, visiting museums, community choruses, dance classes, art classes, mentoring (such as Big Brothers/Big Sisters), gardening classes, soccer...

There's no end to the directions you could go. Look at Meetup.com, for example, for groups in your area on any topic imaginable. Stop at bulletin boards, visit your town library, look at Craigslist under "activities," contact national organizations that interest you to ask about a local chapter, look at lists of events and groups from your town's website or local newspaper. In our times, even people with the quirkiest interests can find others to share with.

If you face severe challenges to your mobility—let's say you live in a remote place and have no money for gas, or you're trapped at home by an abusive partner, or you've got a disability impeding you—of course the process is going to take longer. But you'll find a way. You got your hands on this book, so you must not be completely cut off. Keep working your way toward connection.

Join your neighborhood association, or start one (an internet search for "how to start a neighborhood association" brings you to step-by-step guides)

There's nothing like getting to know people who live near you. I've known of people who have discovered a great potential friend living three houses away whom they had just never happened to meet.

Volunteer for a local board or committee (such as a local conservation group, a food bank, or a women's committee)

Serving in one of these capacities takes volunteering to another level and increases your chance to meet people through giving your time.

2. Pushing existing relationships deeper

It's often true that there are people who are already in our lives to whom we could be closer. Reflect on the people you know and ask yourself:

"Whom could I reach out to more? Is there someone I'd like to spend more time with? How could I get that to happen?"

Ask yourself also:

"Where am I holding back with someone in my life? How could I open up more? How could I offer better support to that person and show them that I'm thinking about them? How could I shift our relationship out of ruts or habits?"

3. Invite people to "split time"

In Part 2, I'll explain the concept of healing partnerships and teach you how to split time; this is a process where you and another person—it can be anyone you like—agree to take turns listening well to each other for an agreed-upon length of time. (We also call this process "co-counseling.") Splitting time is the fundamental way to put the concept of "structured support" into practice and is the centerpiece of the Peak Living Network approach.

One great way to get someone interested in splitting time with you—a friend, a relative, or anyone else you like and respect—is to have them look at PeakLivingNetwork.org, and maybe hand them a printed copy of the section "How to Split Time" (under the "About PLN" tab). It's interesting to observe how many people are quickly interested in splitting time once they learn about it.

4. Take the leap to ask new people to get together with you

Meeting new people doesn't help unless we put ourselves out there to form a friendship. The worst that can happen is that someone can brush us off or tell us that they're too busy. But reaching out feels scary because all kinds of voices run in our heads:

"That person already has tons of friends."

"She's too cool and together."

"She's too smart and interesting."

"People look up to him, why would he want to be friends with me?"

"Everyone already wants to be his friend."

"She barely knows who I am. If I ask her to hang out, it'll be coming out of nowhere."

These voices are expressing *feelings* from earlier injuries, and are just that: feelings. They are not giving valid reasons not to try to make friends with someone. When our inner voices are sending us these kinds of messages, we need to respond with:

"Those are just my feelings. My actions should be based on what I know to be true, drawing upon my deepest self. And the truth is, I can be a really good friend."

When I was in my twenties, I was too afraid to call up new people. So one night I planted myself in a chair with the rule that I couldn't stand up until I had reached out to someone. At the time I wanted be friends with a guy named Bob Gigas whom I considered too cool, confident, and talented for me. But I wasn't going to let those voices control me anymore. I must have been glued to that chair for half an hour, but I finally made that call.

That night was a turning point. The voices didn't stop, but from then on I was able to ignore them and risk reaching out to new people. And Bob became a friend.

I'm struck by how often I'm reading the life story of a famous actor, musician, or writer and I learn that he or she battled loneliness despite having millions of admirers. If only more people had reached out, instead of assuming that the artist was too famous and together for them. *Don't put anyone above you*. Believe in your own value and take risks to connect with people.

Work On Overcoming Fears of Being Close

Letting people into our hearts makes us vulnerable to painful outcomes; there's no denying it. Keeping people at a distance seems safer on the surface. When we let ourselves care about people and allow them to make a difference in our lives, we start to need them; and that means we get hurt if the relationship falls apart or if we lose them for other reasons (one of us moves away, or the person dies, or their life gets too busy).

Close relationships bring up feelings from past emotional wounds; in the words of a wise saying, *"Love reveals what needs to heal."* I'll go so far as to say that if you aren't feeling periodically triggered by your close friends and relatives, you aren't letting anyone in very far.

Love especially tends to trigger feelings from periods in our lives when we were starved for love, were betrayed or dominated by someone we trusted, or felt abandoned (including when a loved one died). These triggers make it challenging to know which of our reactions to a current relationship are really about the present situation and which ones are from the past.

The first step to sorting out whether feelings are from the present or are being triggered from the past is to start observing your own reactions to events. You can train yourself over time to get better and better at knowing which is which. You can't entirely control your emotional reactions, and it isn't even healthful to do so; but you can control what you choose to do when you're upset. (See Chapter 13 under "Living From Choice.")

This understanding means that you can stop allowing your accumulated distress to sabotage your current efforts at closeness. These impediments are not unalterable facts of life enclosing us; they are temporary fences that we will tear down.

Learn to Ask for Help

Modern culture is big on the value of self-reliance. We so often hear individualistic, lonely philosophies such as "You shouldn't need anyone," and, "The only person you can really count on is yourself." They contain a grain of truth, in that over-reliance on other people is unhealthful; we do need confidence that we can handle things ourselves when we have to.

But when we start to believe that handling challenges alone is an obligation, or is the only safe path, we're going astray. *Human beings can't live at their peak except through working together and taking care of each other.*

Try not to assume that other people perceive you as a burden. Most people are eager to help; they *want* to feel needed and useful, they *want* to make a contribution. If they seem reluctant at first, it's usually because they feel cautious about the time commitment they're being drawn into. Once they know they're not being asked to do something overwhelming, they want to be there.

People especially like a sense of mutuality. If you come through for them today, they'll want to come through for you tomorrow. When people reach out for the support they need, everyone benefits, not just the one receiving the assistance.

You can train yourself to ask for help, just as you can train yourself to reach out to form friendships. It's like building a muscle.

Take Care of the People Who Take Care of You

A support system has to be tended and nurtured like a garden. If you draw and draw upon your support system without taking care of it, you will burn it out. Remember to be there for people even while you're going through a hard time yourself. And when you are in such a crisis that you just can't give back, put that time mentally in the bank and give back to people later. Be aware of give and take.

I'm not promoting a miserly habit of keeping track of who exactly has done what, like counting pennies. But maintain an overall sense that you're carrying your weight with people, and if you're not, make adjustments.

Be aware also of not going to your support system over and over again with the same issues. They'll hang in there for a couple of years, but then you'll start to lose them. The fact that you're continually struggling over the same challenges is an indication that it's time to make some changes in your life. (The exception is when you're dealing with an issue that's truly out of your control, such as having a close relative who is incarcerated or seriously ill. Even then it's worth asking yourself, "If there's nothing I can do about this aspect of my life, what other aspects could I take better charge of?")

In the Peak Living Network, we view the building and nurturing of support systems as a lifelong project, always needing our periodic attention. We'll be returning to this undertaking in a number of ways in the chapters ahead. Better and better support is a driving force behind emotional healing and recovery.

Key Points to Remember:

- It is natural to need love and support. Philosophies that teach us that we shouldn't need anything from outside of ourselves are asking us to go against our inherent nature as human beings.

- We don't have to wait and hope for supportive people to come into our lives. We can take charge of building a loving network around ourselves.

- Work to assertively ask for help and generously offer it.

Chapter Eight

The Emotional Immune System

You were built to heal. The human body is a miracle of recovery, facing a never-ending set of health challenges with power, courage, and strategy. Pick up a book about the immune system at a library or book store and flip through it for a few minutes; you'll be amazed by the complexity and the organization of this vast system that is always in motion inside of us.

But here's a fact you're less likely to have heard: Your body also has a plan, closely linked to your immune system, to keep you *emotionally* well.

Your body faces a contradiction. Studies show that *short-term* emotional stress brings a high level of stimulation and immune functioning that is beneficial to your health, but *long-term* stress causes damage to your body.

If you get an intense but quick scare when a growling dog charges you, certain measures of your immune functioning will increase. However, if you become chronically afraid of dogs, developing a preoccupation with being attacked, your immune functioning will *decrease* over time. Your constant fear exhausts your immune system, which can't tolerate being endlessly on alert.

What, then, is best for your health? Your body wants you to *get upset* about things—strong emotions are important to your health—but it doesn't want you to *stay upset* about things. It wants you to feel your fears and sadnesses and outrages, but it also wants you to come back to calm before too long.

Our bodies have a plan to maintain this balance: we have built-in mechanisms for purging painful or distressing emotions once a crisis is *over*—in other words, as soon as the strong negative emotion is no longer essential. Children who are separated from their parents in a crowd cry little or not at all until they're reunited with their caretakers; *then* they start to bawl. People don't tremble much during a scary accident, but once they know they're okay, *that's* when they may start to shake uncontrollably. These are inherent responses as our bodies try to shed distress that we no longer need.

We typically don't, for example, do our deep, productive crying, the kind that comes from the gut, when things are at their worst; the healing kind of crying usually comes when circumstances have gotten a little better—or a lot better.

Our deep bioemotional healing mechanisms are innate; we are born with them. No one has to teach us how to use them. The inherent releases—which together I call "the emotional immune system"—are the following:

- **deep, prolonged crying with tears and periodic sobbing,** which primarily serves to carry away grief and its effects

- **deep, prolonged laughter ("belly laughter"), sometimes accompanied by sweating or shaking,** which primarily serves to carry away embarrassment, lighter fears, and their effects

- **deep, prolonged trembling, whimpering, vocal outbursts (such as "No! No!"), and abrupt physical movement,** which primarily serves to carry away terror and its effects

- **deep prolonged storming, vocal outbursts, and waving or pounding of arms or other abrupt physical movement,** which primarily serves to carry away anger, outrage, and their effects

- **deep, prolonged yawning** (which has a mysterious function but is undeniably part of the emotional immune system, as I explain below)

We were all born with these processes built into us. *If these innate mechanisms had been permitted and supported to operate fully, we would need little else for our emotional healing.* Other approaches to emotional recovery and mental clarity become necessary only because our biologically-based emotional healing processes have been so badly interfered with.

Fortunately, they can be brought back to vibrant functioning.

When these natural channels are re-opened even a little, the benefits are immediate. And when they're brought back to life in a big way, the benefits are transformative.

Crying

The path to healing begins with the human tear. For all of us, crying is the first channel to emotional healing we experienced.

No aspect of human functioning has been more tragically misunderstood. No loyal friend and helper has been more wrongly accused of being a cause of pain. To believe that tears cause suffering is as backwards as to believe that strong tides cause the moon to become full. It is suffering that causes tears; or, to put it more accurately, it is emotional pain that creates the *need* for tears. Our bodies send us tears to wash our sadness away.

The overwhelming majority of people—70% of men and 80% of women—report that they feel better after having a "good cry." Those precious times when we get to weep, sob, or wail, no holds barred, have a bittersweet taste to them. Those deep cries bring a kind of peace that our souls crave, a calm serenity that brings clarity and hopefulness. And that peace comes with a sense of *agency*, the feeling that we're capable of doing what needs to be done in our lives.

Why go through life denying ourselves, each other, and our children opportunities to cry? We don't discourage each other from exercising, eating healthfully, or getting good sleep. Crying is as essential to our well-being—and sometimes as pleasurable—as any of these other ways of caring for ourselves.

The problem is that society has developed an extensive collection of misconceptions about tears (see the box on page 105).

Looking at False Beliefs About Crying

A number of the myths from this box call for closer examination:

"Crying makes you weak." Some people can't think clearly when they cry, as feelings of powerlessness and victimization take over. But the internal collapse is the problem, not the tears, and the two are less connected than they seem. You don't have to stop crying to get stronger; in fact, some people turn their toughest as their tears pour down.

Myths About Crying

- "Crying doesn't do any good."

- "You need to stop people from crying so they'll feel better."

- "Crying leads to weakness (and so is especially bad for males). Resisting tears shows that you're strong."

- "Crying is naughty behavior in children, and must be forbidden."

- "Crying is often used manipulatively."

- "Crying is an inappropriate demand for attention."

- "Crying is a substitute for taking constructive action to improve our lives."

- "It's unnatural for males to cry."

- "Crying that's 'too intense' or 'too long' is a sign of mental health problems."

Superficial hardness is often mistaken for solidity. Children who are ridiculed for their tears learn to put an unfeeling face out to the world; but their core actually gets shakier and shakier. The "manliest" men feel terrified in private and would hate for the world to discover how fragile they feel inside.

The way to raise truly strong boys and girls is to support them and hold them while they cry, gently or wildly, for as long as they need to. Then infuse them with the courage and faith in themselves to go back out there and take on the world.

"Crying doesn't do any good—you have to do something about your problems." This is akin to saying, "Chewing your food doesn't do any good, you have to swallow it." The truth is that we need to cry and take action, and the quality of our action improves when we're getting the healing benefit of tears. It makes no sense to choose between the two.

"Psychologists have established that cathartic approaches to healing don't work." This myth gets repeated as fact, even in psychology books. But research demonstrates the opposite, as I examine in detail in PLN Book 2, The Emotional Immune Response.

"Children use crying manipulatively to get their way." This misconception comes from blaming children for a dynamic that adults create. Adults find it painful or infuriating to hear children cry, so they either give in to the children's demands or start yelling at them for crying. That's our issue, not theirs; we have difficulty listening to them wail because we need to wail. Adults who cry deeply themselves don't go up the wall when children cry.

When a child makes an unreasonable demand and then bursts into tears, lovingly support their feelings *but don't give in to their demands*. The child will do the crying they so much needed, and then will emerge content and cooperative. In the process the child often ends up telling you about an underlying grief that is the real source of distress.

"There's no sense crying over small things." People don't cry over small things, they cry over big ones. When a child or an adult appears to be crying about a trivial matter, a bigger hurt is actually being worked out; the underlying issue will emerge over time. Crying over small things works unconsciously as a safer-feeling way to gradually take apart a large pain.

"Crying just makes it worse.": This statement is false for 75% of the population, as I mentioned above. When people do feel worse after crying, one or more of the following obstacles is present:

- They are crying in unsafe circumstances, such as in the presence of people who are verbally attacking them or who look down upon them for crying.

- They are fighting to hold the tears back.

- Their crying is halting or superficial because their crying channels are blocked in an emotional sense.

- They feel powerless and victimized, and the crying is reinforcing their sense of despair. (In this case, the person probably needs to shift to releasing rage rather than tears for now.)

What Brings On a Good Cry

A deep, cleansing cry is most likely to come at one of the following times:

- when we're feeling loved and supported in our lives overall (even if there isn't anyone there at the moment)

- when someone is holding us

- when we get a reminder of something we went through in the past at a time when we feel safe today (because that same distress is *not* prevalent in our current life)

- when our hearts are holding beautiful images or hopeful thoughts side by side with sad memories

- when we feel the freedom to cry as long and as hard as we need to

"As long and as hard as we need to" is important. We all need a vast number of hours of deep crying. Whenever that channel opens, stay with it for as long as you can.

Tears also come sometimes when we've been intensely physically active for a long time, such as after a long hike, or are sleep-deprived.

One of the implications of the above points is that the better our lives are going, the *more* we may feel like crying. This dynamic can leave people mystified or confused, but it's entirely natural.

Laughter

The saying, "Laughter and crying are the same release," is partly true and partly not. Both laughter and crying bring healing when given the chance to work deeply and at length. But they aren't healing the same wounds, so we need both.

Laughter's role is to relieve and heal fear, particularly fear that doesn't reach a terrifying level, such as:

- the fear that we're going to make fools of ourselves or be laughed at.

- the fear that our brains aren't going to work right.

- the fear of physical injury.

- the fear that people will disapprove of us or dislike us.

These are precisely the fears that most frequently stop us from taking the necessary steps to move forward in our lives. Laughter has a huge untapped potential to help us get unstuck.

When was the last time you reveled in 15 or 20 minutes of real belly laughter? We rarely laugh like that, yet there's almost nothing we enjoy more. We get stopped because laughter, like crying, meets with social disapproval, including:

- we feel that if we laugh "too much" people will think we're unstable.

- we suffered humiliation for laughing when we were kids, with cutting words like, "God, it wasn't that funny," or, "That sure was a dumb joke." We learned that laughing too much is uncool.

- we live in an accomplishment-oriented era where extended laughter is considered a waste of time. The boss says, "All right, folks, let's sober up and get some work done here."

- when our laughter continues for a long time, uncomfortable feelings tend to follow (for reasons that I'll explain later).

- modern society looks down upon children (see Chapter 18), so we avoid "excessive" laughter (and other great childhood habits, such as fantasy play) so that we won't seem childlike.

Next time you're facing a situation that you dread, such as a performance evaluation at work or a gathering with difficult relatives, see if you can provoke a laughing fit before you go. You'll be surprised how much less daunting the task becomes after you release your anxiety in this way.

Laughter plays a role even in the healing of our deepest wounds—events and periods in our lives that were not funny at all—as we'll see.

Fear and Trembling

The natural, healthy response to terror is to flip out; there's no better term to describe it. A person who's been terrified needs to tremble, scream, yelp, yell out, "No! No! No!", and sometimes run around waving their arms. This release usually comes — if it's allowed to — with intermittent periods of crying, raging, and laughing.

A flip-out like this can look kind of insane, but it's actually profoundly healing as long as no one is getting hurt. I'm considered a high-functioning individual, yet in my healing process I've periodically gone to places of terror and grief that would look insane on video. And I feel terrific for days afterwards.

If you experience insane-looking flip-outs sometimes, stop thinking that you harbor a dark secret; you're in good company. If you can let terror, rage, and heartbreak pour out of you in this way, without hurting yourself or scaring anyone, you've broken open a channel to wellness.

When someone is trembling in fear, surrounding people unfortunately tend to quickly hand over a drink "to calm your nerves." The alcohol stops the trembling, and a healing opportunity is missed.

Do reach out for help if you are with someone who is flipping out and any of the following things is true:

- they appear at risk to become violent or self harming

- you know they have a history of violence or self-harm

- you don't feel safe or comfortable to be their support person

However, if you know the person well and they don't have a history of dangerous eruptions, you can leave it up to them whether to call for help or not. If the person says, "I'm okay, I'm just flipping out," stay with them and stay as calm and loving as you can.

As is true of a sobbing cry, the release of terror is a strange and powerful mix of pain and pleasure. A person who is crying their guts out will say that they're in great pain but that they don't want it to stop; it "hurts so good" the way a deep massage does. A person who's having a positive flip-out feels the same way; they're terrified, but roller coaster type terrified, not being-strangled-in-the-dark type terrified, and they can feel how freeing it is.

Raging

Understanding anger release is a little tricky, primarily for one reason: people who behave in destructive ways, such as men who abuse their partners, commonly blame their abusive actions on anger. How do we tell the difference between someone who is genuinely getting anger out and someone being intentionally intimidating?

The answer is surprisingly straightforward; aggressive behavior does not release anger. That's why people who behave in intimidating ways never get any less angry; if anything changes through the years it's that their aggression gets *worse*.

At the same time, I've had many experiences of seeing true anger discharge. The person gets relief and clarity afterwards just as they do from the other inherent releases. Here's what anger looks like when it's truly being released:

- Explosive rage with angry movements, such as pounding pillows, kicking, or waving arms around; furious vocalizations, with or without words, that may be loud but rarely full volume or screaming

- It is usually accompanied by crying before, during, or after.

- The person remains connected to those nearby, as demonstrated by the fact that they periodically stop raging, make eye contact, and perhaps give a brief smile or laugh, before returning to raging.

- The person, although appearing to rage wildly, remains aware of what they're doing; for example, they don't frighten anyone, damage important objects, or disturb people with their screams (if they need to scream, they do so into a pillow).

- The person feels some sense of power, rather than feeling completely hopeless or defeated.

Screaming by itself will rarely release anger; in fact, it tends instead to be a sign of frustration and powerlessness (or of the desire to intimidate).

A certain number of people, most of them women, find that crying doesn't bring them relief. After crying they feel worse than before and may even develop a headache. If this is true of you, focus instead on opening your raging channel. Society has a strong taboo against anger in women that can leave them choking on a mountain of unreleased outrage.

Learning to release rage can have a double benefit, allowing the healing of anger while also loosening the blockage to powerful (as opposed to powerless) crying so that grief can heal.

Men, on the other hand, often need to focus less on their rage and attend more to the healing of grief and fear. In fact, some of what they experience as anger is actually accumulated frustration from the inability to release tears. (I discuss various approaches for men to unblock this channel in *The Healing Partnership: A Manual for Splitting Time* available at PeakLivingNetwork.org.)

Yawning

Even yawning faces social interference. People see it as indicating boredom and therefore rude. Because it is contagious (as all the inherent releases are), it causes other people nearby to yawn, and we hear, "Stop yawning, you're making me sleepy!"

These prohibitions are unfortunate. Yawning doesn't make you sleepy; it actually *increases* energy and mental alertness as long as you stick with it. The first minute or two of yawning can make you realize how tired you already were—that's why people think yawning makes them sleepy—but after that the yawning starts to perk you up.

Try it in your car some time. If you have, say, a 30-minute drive ahead of you and you're feeling low on energy, see if you can keep yourself yawning through the entire trip. You'll feel much less draggy by the time you arrive.

Yawning is mysteriously interwoven with the other innate releases. If, for example, you need a good cry but you're feeling blocked, spending several minutes yawning will sometimes turn the tears loose. Conversely, after a wave of sobbing or belly laughter you may spontaneously break into deep yawns.

The Deepest Releases Come on the Way Up

Depressed people have been observed to cry very little. Our deepest laughter, crying, and other innate releases don't tend to happen when we're feeling our worst; they swing into action after we've endured pain or stress but the conditions have started to improve. They function most commonly when our awareness is roughly balanced between a source of pain and a source of reassurance. For example, we tend to cry harder if someone is holding us; feeling safe and loved in this way balances out our feelings of isolation or grief, allowing the crying to pour forth.

If you experience an unexpected burst of tears or laughter, the cause is often that a cross-current of feelings had suddenly formed inside you. Strong positive feelings side-by-side with a source of distress stimulate our healing processes.

Even yawning happens more as our situation improves; a study years ago found that hospital patients yawn more frequently as they move into the upswing of their physical recovery.

The Common Characteristics of Innate Releases

The innate bioemotional releases share distinct elements showing that they make up an integrated and natural healing system:

1) They're built into our bodies, and thus do not have to be learned; they are exhibited spontaneously by even the youngest children.

2) They function most commonly and deeply after a cri-

sis has passed, not during it (though they will sometimes come during a crisis also).

3) They function more deeply in a person who is feeling safe, loved, and supported and who is in physical contact with another person.

4) They're contagious.

5) They're uncomfortable or even painful, yet we wish for them to continue (if they're really flowing).

6) They're interwoven; deep release in any of the five forms (crying, laughter, raging, trembling, or yawning) commonly leads to eruptions of one of the other forms. A person who is releasing emotions deeply and for an extended period will commonly *cycle* among the different forms of release without any effort to do so.

7) When these releases are allowed to function deeply, they lead to dramatically improved spirits, mental clarity, hopefulness, and energy. They lead us to find solutions to problems where none seemed possible before. Over time, they can heal even the deepest wounds; their healing power exceeds that of any other path to emotional recovery.

Closing Thoughts

In *The Healing Partnership* (which is free on the PLN website), and in *The Emotional Immune Response*, I offer many strategies for increasing our access to deep discharge in these natural forms, unblocking our release channels. The main points to focus on for now are the following:

- When you experience laughter, crying, or any of the

innate releases, try to keep the discharge going rather than making it stop. See if you can actually go deeper; conscious attention toward this goal is sometimes all it takes to free our releases.

- Look for opportunities to increase laughter and crying in your daily life.

- As you start to practice splitting time (which we take up in the next chapter), look for ways to use that process to bring more emotional release into your life.

- When you are in a tough spot in your day (or week, or month) experiment with a quick round of crying or laughter. Although I've been emphasizing the power of longer bouts of release, you may be surprised by the ability that even just a few minutes' worth can have to bounce you out of an emotional rut.

Two Cautionary Notes:

1) Chemically-induced releases don't work. People can sob for hours drunk or on drugs and nothing gets released; they don't arrive at mental clarity or emotional relief, and are just as likely to be intoxicated the next night. By contrast, you'll see almost immediate life changes from deep releasing without drugs or alcohol.

2) Laughter from hearing oppressive jokes doesn't heal either. When people spend an evening laughing at a racist stand-up comedian, they come out more hateful than when they went in. It appears that participating in oppression is its own type of altered state, like being drunk or on drugs, that somehow blocks the release processes from functioning.

One Last Hopeful Insight:

Due to the way our stored distresses are interwoven, any time you make progress healing from a painful event or period in life, you are *simultaneously* healing important pieces of distress from earlier wounds. This is true whether or not you are conscious of it. Thus any time we're healing successfully, the entire rigid structure that holds us back is starting to crumble, and our freedom is growing.

Key Points to Remember:

- Our bodies have a plan for keeping us emotionally well, not just physically well.

- When these channels are working well, they bring us the deepest healing.

- We can regain our access to these channels even if they feel blocked currently.

- When these channels are truly working, we need little else for our healing.

Part Two

Healing Together: The End of Self-Help

Chapter Nine

Healing Partnerships

Human beings have lived in complex societies for a million years, the drive for interaction and cooperation running to the core of our nature, as fundamental as any characteristic we have. To be at our best we need to work, think, play, and live near people we care about and trust.

Even the healing of our bodies is tied to our communities. Researchers have found, for example, that people who feel part of a supportive network have greater rates of recovery from immune-related diseases such as cancer, while those that experience the greatest isolation succumb most quickly. Emotional healing, too, works far better when it's a collective effort.

Most of our deepest wounds involve times when we were left to cope with painful events alone. And this is precisely why "self-help" doesn't work; it leaves us once again in solitary battle with our difficulties.

The foundational activity of the Peak Living Network is the creation of **healing partnerships**, in which two people work together to support progress for both of them. This relationship is highly structured; it isn't just like friends getting together to talk.

Healing partners share structured, focused attention, which we refer to as **splitting time** or **co-counseling**. Partners take turns listening to each other for extended periods of time without interrupting. While it's one person's turn to talk, the other person listens with undivided attention, offering support but never shifting to talking about himself or herself. Half way through the time the two *switch roles*, with the person who had been speaking becoming the support person for the second half.

Healing partners split all different lengths of time, depending on their needs and schedules. You might split ten minutes on the phone one day, split twenty minutes two days after that, and then three days later meet in person for a two-hour session, with each of you taking a turn of nearly an hour. Short and long periods of focused attention contribute to healing in different ways and are both important.

When it's your turn to be the speaker you don't necessarily literally speak during your whole turn, but you're always *the focus of attention*. You may opt to sit quietly and feel your feelings, write in your journal, ask your partner to hold you while you cry, or lie down near your partner and sleep. All of these you would do with your healing partner's aware, loving attention.

Splitting time may sound like therapy; in fact we often refer to the listener as the "counselor" and the speaker as the "client." But it's actually quite different, because:

- it's *free*—no money is exchanged.

- it's *mutual*—both people act as the healer and the healed, taking turns between those two roles.

- it's based in *a different set of beliefs about where healing comes from* than most professional therapy is.

- most people find it considerably *more powerful* than professional therapy.

In the Peak Living Network we work to develop a high level of skill in how we work with each other, and we reach for deep, transformative healing; in these ways (and others) our work is distinct from what is known as "peer counseling." PLN offers various resources to help everybody in the network steadily become more knowledgeable and effective counselors for each other.

Moreover, the better you get at skillfully supporting another person's healing, the better your own recovery goes; the two processes work far better when they're interwoven.

Terminology for Splitting Time

Terms on the left are equivalent to terms on the right:

Healing partnership	=	Co-counseling relationship
Listener	=	Counselor
Speaker	=	Client
Splitting time	=	Co-counseling, doing a co-counseling session
My healing partner	=	My co-counselor
Splitting short chunks of time	=	Doing a mini-session

You may need to try splitting time with a few people before you find a partner that is a good fit for you; I'll guide you through the process of choosing someone to work with.

When two individuals start to co-counsel regularly they

get better and better at offering each other support that really *works*, learning the specifics of each other's healing needs. They also build confidence and trust in one another, so that each one starts to have the wonderful feeling, "My partner is really there for me."

Over time, healing partners come even to love each other, based on mutual understanding and shared healing. Growing and healing is a pleasure unlike any other, and it is even greater when we have a loving companion in the process who is walking the same road.

A healing partnership can be brief or long-lived. I have had some powerful experiences where I only split time with a person once, yet the interaction had a lasting and beautiful effect on me. At the other end of the spectrum, I have had a few people that I have split time with regularly, including one dear healing partner with whom I did a two-hour session (one-hour turns for each of us) every week without fail for over five years.

Your can split time over the phone, and to some extent you can even share support by email, but in-person sessions will be the most powerful.

Finding a Healing Partner

You can build a healing partnership with *anyone* who listens well, or who is open to learning how to do so. The ideal partner for you, though, is someone:

- whom you like and enjoy.

- whose way of living you respect and admire.

- who gives you energy, who has some hopefulness about life.

- who isn't among your closest friends or relatives and isn't your lover/life partner.

- whom you don't work closely with at your job.

- who lives close enough to you that you can do some or all of your sessions in person.

None of these is a requirement. Some people find that splitting time with their life partner works quite well, for example. You also don't have to choose just one healing partner; I've had times in life when I was co-counseling regularly with as many as four different people, getting valuable things out of my sessions with each person.

I do recommend finding at least one healing partner who isn't among your close friends or relatives, because you'll feel safer to open up with someone who isn't in your social life. Plus you'll be able to more reliably count on the person to be there for you, whereas relationships with friends and lovers always have their periods of conflict or distance.

Seek out a person whose strengths you can see, so that each of you gains inspiration from the other; if you split time with someone you feel sorry for, he or she will gradually come to feel like a drain on you. A healing relationship needs to be balanced and mutual.

If someone comes to mind with whom you would like to work, print out the "PLN Principles" from PeakLivingNetwork.org to give to them, and encourage them to do further reading on the website. Many people feel excited when they learn about healing partnerships and emotional support networks, and are eager to give the ideas a try; with a little luck the person you have in mind will react that way.

If no one in your present life comes to mind, here are some avenues you can take:

- Go on PeakLivingNetwork.org and click on the "Find Healing Partners" tab. Then choose "General Co-counseling Partners."

- You'll be asked to share a little information about yourself and describe any preferences you have in choosing a partner (a woman or a man, someone close to you in age, someone who lives in your area so that you can work in person, and similar requests you might make).

- Place a notice on Craigslist or other online bulletin board stating that you're interested in finding someone who has read *The Joyous Recovery* or perused the Peak Living Network website who would be interested in working with you on applying the principles.

- Ask at your town library for other strategies that people use in your area to find activity partners who share a particular interest (such as Meetup.com).

- Start a book group in your town to read and discuss *The Joyous Recovery* a chapter at a time. As you get to know people in your group you can see which person you might like to approach about working one-on-one. (To learn more, click on "Book Groups" at PeakLivingNetwork.org.)

- Start a support group in your town on PLN principles, and choose a possible healing partner among people who come to the group (see "Local Groups" at PeakLivingNetwork.org)

- You can take a Peak Living Network training course (click on "About PLN" on the website and then click on "Training Courses").

Caution!

Any time you are considering splitting time with someone whom you don't already know, meet with him or her in a public place first. You might also consider asking for a personal reference. Avoid anyone who seems to be rushing you to meet in private before you're comfortable doing so. Take the same precautions as you would when meeting someone on an online dating site.

The Growth of the Healing Partnership

Learning to be effective counselors for each other takes time and involves breaking some longstanding habits. It also takes time to build trust between two people. Focus on being there for each other, compassionate and stalwart, week after week. You will both see the impact on your lives before long.

Confidentiality

Unless the speaker gives explicit permission otherwise, anything that is said in the context of splitting time is to go nowhere else. Trust can't be built in the absence of confidentiality. Keep confidentiality even with respect to issues that seem trivial; you can never be sure which parts of what your client shares could have connections to serious wounds.

In the Peak Living Network, we extend confidentiality further: We ask that, once the speaker's turn is over, you not make reference to anything the person spoke about *even in speaking to that person*. We work hard to remember never to comment in any way on the person's session. The only exception is when your partner specifically asks you to check back about a particular issue (as in, "Could you ask me next week how I'm doing with this?").

This extension to confidentiality is powerful because it gives the person speaking complete control over everything they have chosen to reveal. That means that when they expose a feeling, an event, or a vulnerability, they're exposing it *only for that moment*; they don't have to worry that they're going to hear about it from you another time which might be the wrong time. The result is that people are able to do deep work more quickly. *Get in the habit of never bringing up anything from somebody's turns once that turn is over.*

When Maintaining Confidentiality Feels Wrong

There's one exception to confidentiality: Don't burden yourself with secrets that are too much to handle, such as serious suicidal urges or recent child abuse. Consult with an experienced person from PLN or with a mental health professional about the situation, after first informing your healing partner that you need to do so.

Choosing a "Supervisor"

Any healing partnership can mutually agree to a third person to go to for advice or ideas about your work together. That person is called the "supervisor" for the two of you even though that person is a peer (as we all are in PLN). By choosing a supervisor, you and your partner give yourselves a way to get advice and support without breaking confidentiality. (You can read more about the role of the supervisor in *The Healing Partnership* manual which is free to read on the website.)

Keep to a Clearly Defined Relationship

Healing partnerships are most powerful when they honor their original purpose. Unless you and your partner were friends before you began splitting time, I recommend that you not socialize. Engaging in a healing process together can make you feel very close, so the pull to be friends or lovers is often potent. But you're both vulnerable because you've exposed your emotions to each much more rapidly than friends normally do; plus it's easy to idealize each other since you've only seen each other in the most loving circumstances. This all adds up to a context where socializing can lead easily to feeling hurt by the other person and thus for relationships to rupture and be lost.

If you split time together for a full year and find that you still want to have a social relationships, there is a cautious process that I recommend for making the transition; you can read the details in *The Healing Partnership*. (None of this applies if you were already friends or romantic partners before you started splitting time.)

Sex and Splitting Time Don't Mix

Sexual contact is not appropriate in the context of meeting to split time, whether before, during, or after the actual session. Sexual contact or advances are also not appropriate at any Peak Living Network gathering and people who engage in them will be asked to leave.

You can't reliably use good judgment about what kind of sexual intimacy would be good for you while in the midst of opening up deep, powerful, and often painful feelings. The nature of splitting time and of other PLN activities — the rapid emotional closeness, the focused and loving attention, the vulnerability, the supportive physical affection — can make you feel that the other person is the most loving and accepting person you've ever met; in other words, it's easy to attach all of our unmet needs from the past to an individual we come to know in this context. And then having sex with them starts to feel like it would fill all of our empty places.

I have never seen sexual contact lead to good results in the context of emotional healing work. The actual result is that people wind up feeling regretful, triggered, used, reinjured, or all of these at once. (And don't ever buy it if someone tries to convince you that sexual contact with them will help you heal your sexual issues — it won't.)

The other side of all this is that we can be delightfully physically affectionate with each other, in a way that is very supportive of our healing, if we:

1) watch carefully for what is wanted and what is unwanted, and respect each other's wishes and limits

2) don't cross the boundary into sexual contact or anything that could be interpreted as sexual contact

Sexuality is a wonderful aspect of life. But it doesn't belong here except as a subject for people to work on — without actual sexual contact — during their turns.

Splitting Time Between Close Friends or Intimate Partners

Splitting time with a friend or lover can work well, especially if it's in *addition* to sessions you do regularly with someone who isn't in your social life. I offer three guidelines for splitting time in this context:

1) Don't enter a session with bad feelings towards each other, as there won't be any real sense of safety and the time will be wasted. If you have issues to resolve between the two of you, do so before you begin splitting time.

2) Keep track of which things you have learned about each other in sessions and which things you have learned through normal conversation. Don't bring up anything you heard while splitting time with the person; your social relationship and your co-counseling relationship need to be kept separate.

3) During your turn don't work on issues or tensions you have regarding the person you're splitting time with (unless you've made an agreement *before the session began* that it's okay to do so). Putting your friend or lover in a position of not being allowed to respond—because of the structure of splitting time—to things you are saying about him or her can lead to deepening tension and injury in your relationship.

Making a Healing Partnership Work for You

Once you've found a healing partner who feels like a good fit for you, there are many ways to maximize the benefits of splitting time:

- **Break through barriers to asking for what you need.** If there is a particular type of support you want from your partner, speak up about it. You can request more validation, to receive certain reminders, or to get particular kinds of encouragement. Similarly, make it known if your partner is interfering in any way, whether by talking too much, giving advice, or being overly passive and quiet.

- **Be committed to your healing partner.** Show up on time for sessions, don't cancel or shorten them except for emergencies, and don't interrupt them to take phone calls or check texts. (Phones should be off during sessions.) Make your partner feel that you value him or her and value your meetings.

- **Accept and welcome discomfort and upheaval.** Leading a fulfilling life requires sailing in turbulent—but more beautiful—waters. Gauge your quality of life by how *satisfied* you feel inside, rather than by how superficially content or comfortable you are. Take risks; your healing processes are stimulated when you step outside of behavioral ruts that are based on habits, old wounds, and the fear of change. (We'll look at this in more detail in the chapters ahead.)

- **Avoid substances that numb feelings.** Alcohol and drugs, including nicotine and caffeine, are suppressive to emotional healing. Even excessive use of sweets dulls emotions and short-circuits internal processing. Reduce or eliminate your use of these numbing substances, beginning by making sure you aren't using them every day, and keep them well away from your co-counseling sessions.

- **Do what needs to be done.** Everything goes better when we get in the habit of pushing ourselves through fear and discouragement to take care of what is urgent. Get support for yourself, such as splitting a few minutes with a healing partner on the phone, both before and after taking difficult steps. If you gather adequate resource in this way, you can live outside of your comfort zone—and love it—day after day.

- **Read *The Healing Partnership*.** This complete manual for splitting time is available free online at PeakLiving-Network.org. You can also order a print copy on the website if you prefer.

Using the Telephone

You can split any length of time over the phone. Whenever you feel the need you can call your healing partner or anyone else you know from the Peak Living Network and ask, "Are you free to split some time?" Then agree how long you can spend and divide the time in half. In the next chapter, I'll explain the details of how to split time over the phone.

Quick phone sessions are especially valuable before or after important events. Let's say that you're dreading an upcoming confrontation with a difficult co-worker. So, a half hour beforehand, you call your healing partner and ask for five minutes to talk and laugh about your anxiety. You'll be amazed at the way that even such a short dose of loving attention leaves you feeling much stronger and more able to take on the conflict and get it over with. By integrating support into our lives in this way we find that we can take things on that we were tempted to put off, stand up for ourselves better, and take the sting out of difficult events.

When you are in the listening role in a phone session, follow the same guidelines that you would in person. Don't shift the subject to yourself or drift into conversation, but do offer brief supportive comments, caring, and appreciation.

Being Present at Special Challenges

You can ask your healing partner to be present at crucial times when you need extra support and attention. You might be facing a frightening medical procedure, having to testify at court, or going home for the first time in years to confront an abusive parent. At these times, your partner can accompany you to assist you in processing emotions before and after the event and to support you during it.

Continue to follow the principle of equal effort, so that the time your co-counselor spends supporting you at a time like this is repaid through session time that you give them (or through similar support for them with an actual life challenge).

Splitting Time Creatively

A talking-and-feeling session is not always what you most need. For example, if you're having chronic sleep difficulties you might benefit more from what we call "guarded rest," where you lie down or sleep while your partner continues to give you full attention. If you have a scary phone call that you've been avoiding, you might make that call right during your turn while your partner encourages and supports you in person. If you have a phobia about balancing your checkbook, bring it to your session one day and work on it during your turn. If you're an artist, see what it's like to engage in your artwork with the warm, focused attention of your co-counselor. These creative ways of using session time are valuable in themselves, plus they sometimes set deep healing work into motion.

Saying Goodbye to a Healing Partner

A healing partnership, like all relationships, can come to an end. One of you may move out of town, or your schedules may change so they are no longer compatible, or your needs in a partner might change. Honor the importance and sensitivity of what you have shared by communicating clearly about the ending rather than just dropping out of each other's lives. If one person wants to continue and the other does not there may be some hurt feelings, and these are best expressed and dealt with rather than avoided. A clean ending will help both of you to move positively into your next co-counseling relationship.

When you get together to split time for the last time, take turns sharing what each of you has appreciated about the other. Celebrate the ways you have been helpful to one other and the accomplishments you each have had over the period you've been meeting.

Understanding the Power of a Healing Partnership

I have had many healing partners over the thirty-plus years that I have been splitting time with people. Several of these people (I've listed them in the Acknowledgments) have been as precious to me as any friend or lover and their impact on my life has been as great.

I encourage you to begin right away to explore what a healing partnership can do. You may be surprised by the leap forward in how much you feel held and supported in the world, and by the way your progress rockets forward. At its best a co-counseling relationship can propel you to a completely new level of satisfaction and fulfillment in life, lifting you toward the peak.

And the more that you and your partner get involved in the Peak Living Network—by going to open support meetings, by reading the publications, by participating in the online forums, and being part of other PLN activities— the more your sessions together will take off, as both of you draw energy, inspiration, and skill from your healing community.

Key Points to Remember:

- "Structured support" begins with the creation of healing partnerships.

- Healing partnerships primarily function by splitting time, also called "co-counseling."

- Splitting time is the driving force of the Peak Living Network approach to healing. Making it part of your weekly or even daily practice will create more of a leap forward for your healing than almost any other step you could take.

Chapter Ten

The Structure of a Co-Counseling Session

Splitting time is the fundamental activity that undergirds the Peak Living Network. It's a way to dramatically improve the focus and the quality of listening that we offer to each other and is a life-changing practice when we build it regularly into our lives. It's usually done in pairs, but can also be done in a threesome and in fact works in any size of group.

When we split time, we commit to giving each other the highest quality of warm, respectful attention that we're capable of. The time available is divided in half. During the first half, one person gives undivided attention while the other person speaks—or sits quietly, or writes, or cries, or whatever they find most useful to do that day while receiving caring attention. Then the two people *switch roles* for the second half, with the listener becoming the speaker and the speaker becoming the listener.

Two people can split any length of time; a session could last six minutes (three-minute turns each) or it could last two hours (one-hour turns each). A three-minute turn with another person's loving attention can have a surprising impact on your day; there is no amount of time that's too short to be worth splitting. Time can be split in person or over the phone. You'll find, naturally, that you do a different kind of work in a turn that's just a few minutes long than you would in a full hour, and talking on the phone is not the same as having someone in your physical presence. These different kinds of sessions serve distinct but equally valuable purposes.

If you want to see your healing really move, make space in your life for a session at least once a week of between an hour and a half and two hours, so that each person gets at least a 45-minute turn and ideally 50 or 55. A session of this length permits each person to work into thoughts and feelings at a useful and powerful depth. In addition, build two or three short sessions into your week of just ten or fifteen minutes total (five or so minutes for each person). These "mini-sessions" will typically be done by phone for practical reasons.

Choosing a Space

Most in-person sessions take place in people's homes, for convenience and comfort, but they may also take place outdoors or in any private space that's available to you. Choose a space that is as attractive and uncluttered as possible; people have an easier time doing healing work when their physical surroundings reflect hopefulness and coziness, and where there are pleasing things to look around at such as plants, pictures on the walls, or crafts.

Look for a spot where both people can be comfortable. A couch, a floor with mats or cushions, or a bed (especially in the corner of a room) can all be set up to allow both people to have back support but also to sit close together. Sitting near each other in chairs is an okay fallback but tends to feel more distant.

The host should make tissues and water available. However, the focus should be on the session rather than on hosting or socializing, so it's best not to offer food or other drinks and just get down to the business of splitting time.

The Essential Format

Step 1: Choose Who Goes First And Set A Timer

Begin by agreeing to the length of turns you are each going to take. Unless each person's turn is going to be twenty minutes or less, allow for about a five minute break between turns to stretch, use the bathroom, get a drink of water, and mentally prepare to switch roles. So, for example, if you have two hours total, that gives each of you a 55-minute turn with a short break in between.

If one person has a preference to go first you can choose turns on that basis, and otherwise flip a coin. Each time you meet subsequently, switch off which person goes first unless one of you has a strong preference otherwise.

Decide how the time is going to be kept. It can be distracting to the speaker if the listener keeps checking the time, so it's best to set an audible timer. Buying a small hand-held cooking timer is a good investment rather than using a phone timer, so that you keep your mind off of your phone. Set the timer to go off five minutes before the person's turn ends to allow time to wrap up the session.

Phones need to be kept turned off and out of reach during sessions. It's not acceptable to take calls or check messages while you're in the counseling role, no matter how briefly. The speaker can choose to be reachable during his or her turn but I strongly recommend against it; that's an important habit to break so that you give your full attention to your healing.

The speaker, or "client," is the ultimate decision-maker during his or her time; this is a crucial distinction between a co-counseling session and a therapy session. During your turn the time belongs entirely to you, and the listener should never pressure you in any way about how to use your turn (though non-pressuring questions and suggestions are fine).

At the same time, the listener needs to *take charge decisively* of the structure of the session. The listener should begin by setting the timer, turn his or her full attention to the client, and begin to guide the session through the phases described below. Avoid moving timidly when you're the listener; if the speaker feels the need to diverge from the usual structure that day it's up to him or her to say so.

Think of the speaker as the owner of a shop and the listener as the manager. The owner has the final say, but at the same time wants the manager to take clear charge of running things; the owner can step in at any point and say that things need to be done differently, but the rest of the time wants the confidence of knowing that the manager is handling things decisively.

Step 2: Focus First On Positive Developments

It is the listener's job to begin right away by asking the opening questions, which should be about positive events or feelings from the client's recent life. Ask things such as:

"So, what are a few things that have gone well lately?"

"What have you felt happy about in the last few days?"

"What can you take pride in from recent things you've done?"

"What's new and good?"

It makes an important difference to the speaker when the listener takes clear charge of starting the session by asking one of these questions, establishing from the beginning that the listener is fully present and wants to hear about the speaker's life.

This "new and good" phase of a session gives the speaker a lift, providing strength and safety with which to approach more difficult feelings and issues further on in the turn. Try to celebrate triumphs—even small ones—and to tap into sources of pride and hope. If you are the speaker and at first you feel that nothing's been good lately, take a little time and find something to be positive about, however trivial it may seem at the moment. It's important to break out of the habit of taking an "it's all so impossibly hard" attitude towards our lives *even when in many ways things really are that bad*; deep work is unlikely to happen unless you first anchor yourself in some positive aspects of life.

If you are doing a full-length session, the counselor should encourage the client to spend at least five minutes on these positive points. For a shorter session, always take at least a minute or two on this phase.

It's valuable to occasionally spend your *entire turn* celebrating positive developments, with your partner's attention helping you to take it all in. Don't worry about "spending too long on the good stuff."

Step 3: Give Brief Attention To Minor Challenges

When the speaker feels finished reporting on the good news, the listener moves the session to the next phase, where we check in about smaller issues or distractions that may be on the speaker's mind. Ask questions such as:

"Have there been any smaller hard things lately?"

"Is anything on your mind that could make it hard to be fully present today?"

"Have you had any minor upsets?"

   We pay some brief attention to these concerns to help the speaker lay them aside, making it easier to turn attention to the central issues he or she wants to focus on. This phase also gives time for the speaker to absorb the caring presence of the listener before wading into more difficult waters.

Step 4: The Heart Of The Session

Next it's time for the listener to ask: "Is there something you'd like to focus on today?" This question introduces the main phase of the session which continues until only a few minutes remain in the speaker's turn.
   The speaker is the sole decider of what he or she wants to work on. The subject need not always be a hard one; some days the speaker may want to discuss gardening, music, or soccer, or might opt to just sit quietly while receiving attention or being held. Her time belongs to her, and she decides what is most important for her healing that day.
   When you are the listener, support your client fully and encourage her to give space to the feelings that arise inside of her, noticing them and sitting with them. Ask the speak-

er questions from time to time that guide her toward her emotions; often asking simply, "How does that feel?" will be adequate. If she rushes past an emotional place, invite her to pause for a moment and just notice what's going on inside her, so that she doesn't bury her feelings in words.

If the client starts to discharge emotions, support that release and make it the highest priority of the session. Tune in also to whether the client is wanting to have you sit closer or hold her, and to any other way you can contribute to her sense of safety and support; you'll learn many techniques in the next chapter.

Step 5: Get The Speaker Re-Rooted In The Positive Present

When there are about five minutes left in the speaker's turn, the listener moves the session into the final phase, working to bring the speaker's awareness back to the present moment and to positive thoughts. The goal is to help the speaker avoid going through the remainder of his day weighed down by the heavier aspects of life which he has opened himself up to during the session. Assist him to turn his attention away from the past and away from his sources of fear or sadness, aiming it out into the present-time world.

During this phase, the listener does one or more of the following:

- asks the speaker, "What are you looking forward to?"
- points the speaker's attention toward his five senses, asking questions along the lines of:
  - "Tell me four green things you can see in this room."
  - "Name as many different sounds as possible that you can hear right now."

- "Tell me three of your favorite things to eat, and why you like them."
- asks entertaining trivia questions
- invites the speaker to look at a book of photography or humor
- tries any other ideas that are light or fun

During this phase avoid making any references to what has gone on in the speaker's turn that day, such as saying, "you went into some really deep places" or "you did some great work today." The last few minutes are for looking forward into life, not backward into the session that is now ending, and even praise about the session can cast the speaker back into his or her distress.

There's another reason not to praise people for the work they do in a session: In our times we've become overly focused on accomplishing things, to the exclusion of living life for the pleasure of living. Let's not turn our healing processes into another accomplishment.

Be aware of how your client is doing as the session is wrapping up. If he still seems to be stuck in the feelings he's been processing, take a couple of extra minutes on these "attention out" activities that I've just described. Make sure he is fully present before ending his turn.

Step 6: Switch To The Other Person

When the first person's turn is over, take a break for a few minutes and then switch roles for the remaining half of the time.

Shorter Sessions

When splitting quick periods of time, say five or ten minutes per person, you may shorten the "new and good" phase to just a minute or so, and you may decide to skip the minor concerns phase altogether. On days when your feelings are raw and available you might skip even the "new and good" portion and dive right into expressing or releasing what you're feeling. But most of the time stick to the discipline of starting your turn with at least one quick piece of positive news.

As with a full session, make sure the speaker is back in the present before saying good-bye. You'll spend less time on this "turning attention back to the present" phase than in a full-length session—perhaps just a minute—but the return to lighter subjects remains important.

When the two of you have only a few minutes available, you may decide to let one person take the whole time, with the agreement that the listening time will be returned on another occasion. Keep rough track of what is owed, though, because over time it's essential that listening be shared equally.

The Listener's Role

Even though we often refer to the listener as the "counselor," you don't act as analyst or therapist when you're in that role. Your job is to guide the session through its different phases, but not to suggest what the speaker should focus on nor to offer interpretations of the speaker's issues. Concentrate on being supportive, keeping your awareness firmly on the speaker. Avoid talking about yourself, even as a way of expressing understanding or common ground (as in, "I've been through that too," for example). There are many ways demonstrate to the speaker that you get what she's saying that don't involve shifting the focus to yourself, as we will see.

Steer strictly away from advice-giving and problem-solving; allow the speaker to come to her own solutions, which will emerge of their own accord once she has had time to do the emotional processing and releasing that she needs. Never offer suggestions except when the speaker *specifically asks* for them.

The Speaker's Role

When it's your turn, give some thought to what will be the most valuable way to use your time that day. Try to choose just one or two issues to focus on so that you don't run lightly over the surface and miss out on deeper work. Use the listener's support as a source of strength, but don't expect him or her to fix things for you; a successful session occurs when the listener and the speaker are *both* thinking carefully about how to help the listener heal.

Work hard in sessions, while also taking occasional time to rest or pursue entertaining subjects. If tears or other releases come to the surface stick with them, for they are the flower and fruit of a session. Avoid the temptation to hurry past the release and return to talking, which may feel more comfortable but is far less transforming.

Consider bringing things to sessions that help you process feelings, such as your journal (either to write in it for a few minutes or to read portions aloud that you're comfortable sharing), photographs that evoke happy or sad emotions in you, or a piece of music that has a powerful impact on you.

Three-Person and Group Sessions

Sessions can also be done with three people or more. Simply divide the time equally among the participants. Each person decides during his turn which of the others will be his primary counselor. The additional people are welcome to make supportive comments or ask questions, but the primary counselor is responsible to move the session through its phases and take the lead on the counseling.

It's important to choose a primary counselor; I've observed repeatedly that people who avoid doing so end up less connected to their emotions during their turn because they don't have a focal point within the group's attention. The power of the group's attention becomes greater, not less, when the speaker chooses a lead counselor.

Why This Session Structure is Important

One of the great challenges of recovery is that we don't heal well when we spend too much time dwelling on the more painful aspects of life, but we also don't progress if we avoid them. The Peak Living Network approach thus takes a third way, where:

- we regularly set aside substantial time to delve thoroughly and with full focus into our emotions, no holds barred, in a safe and supportive context where healing can really happen.

- the rest of the time we work hard to live as fully *outside* of those distresses as we possibly can, knowing that we have time reserved (ideally each week) for attending to them.

This approach contrasts sharply with philosophies of healing that encourage people to spend a lot of time ruminating on old issues or sitting with painful feelings. Healing actually works best when we avoid the middle ground, being sort of in our pain and sort of not; it's far more effective to dive in wholeheartedly, including releasing pain as deeply as we can, and then to leave it all thoroughly aside until next time.

The concept of "the joyous recovery" is lived out right here. Through following the Peak Living Network approach, we can live lives of happiness and satisfaction even right while we're dealing with heavy injuries from our past.

Key Points to Remember:

- Following a clear structure and really sticking to it brings great rewards when two people are splitting time. Even if rules and guidelines annoy you a little, give this process a serious and disciplined effort. You'll be glad you did.

- Understanding the reasoning behind these guidelines will help you integrate them into your practice.

- There is plenty of room for experimentation and creativity in the co-counseling process. The structure doesn't need to hold you back in any way.

Chapter Eleven

Splitting Time for Deep, Transformational Healing

Emotional injuries from the past, even the deepest ones, can truly heal. Learning how to do deep work in your one-on-one sessions is a gateway to transformation.

The Keys to the PLN Counseling Approach

In the Peak Living Network, we practice a collection of ways of being there for each other that are distinctive. Learning these counseling techniques helps you to take the power of your listening to another level, where you help propel your partner's healing. There is no formula for when to use a particular technique; through experience and experimentation you'll develop an intuitive sense of what to try.

Validation

Validating the speaker's feelings is the essential first step. It can be as simple as saying, "That must have been a painful experience for you," or, "You had every right to be upset." Simple human compassion is a powerful tool.

Another way to offer validation is to try to reflect back succinctly in your own words what you've heard your client say, thereby letting her know that you've grasped what she's expressing. For example:

Listener: **It sounds like you could never feel sure what your father was going to do next, and that created a lot of anxiety for you.**

Reflecting aloud in this way also gives the speaker an opportunity to explain the feeling further or to clarify. In the example above, the speaker might reply, "Yes, but it wasn't as much that I got anxious as that I became resentful." This kind of fine-tuning in the communication between the two of you helps the speaker feel that you're taking it all in.

Expressing Interest and Acceptance

Ask questions that show your desire to learn about the speaker's experience. For example, if the speaker says a little bit about something he went through but then stops, you might say:

Listener: **I'd really like to know what that whole thing was like for you.**

During a time when he takes a long pause, you might ask:

Listener: **What's the thought you're having right now?**

If you think your client is censoring something, encourage him to go ahead and share the thought. Reassure him that you won't think less of him from learning the truth about what's going on inside him.

Appreciation

Let the speaker know the things that you appreciate about her. Notice the things that she does well, the ways that she thinks clearly, and the things that she cares deeply about, and reflect those things back to her.

Be alert for cues about the ways she feels self-critical, and see if you can make supportive comments that help to thwart those critical voices. For example, if she's being hard on herself about how she handled a recent challenge in her life, you might say:

Listener: **You're a good person, and you don't deserve to beat yourself up about things. You did the best you could in incredibly difficult circumstances.**

Remember, though, that the goal of your comments is to help her feel supported in her feelings, *not* to talk her out of feeling them.

Guiding the Speaker Toward Self-Appreciation

Encourage the speaker to tell you about the things he's good at, the people he has loved well, the things he's physically capable of. He has done miraculously well in the face of the challenges the world has presented him with, though he may well not feel that way today. Taking pride out loud helps him to notice his own strengths, and contradicts the societal taboo against feeling good about himself.

Taking Stands

Although being critical of the speaker will almost never be helpful, positive judgments are great and sometimes crucial. In particular, let your partner know what you believe about the way the world should be and the way people deserve to be treated.

For example, when someone describes something that happened to her that was clearly unjust, you might say:

Listener: **You should never have been treated that way; that was completely wrong.**

You can go further and tell your partner how things should have been:

Listener: **People should have been there for you, and they should have listened to you about what was happening to you. You should have been taken seriously!**

Notice when the speaker blames herself for things that have happened to her, and see if you can point out ways that those events were not her fault. Help her also to forgive herself for her own past reactions, especially in childhood, to bad things that were happening, as in:

Listener: **It's perfectly understandable that you got in a with a bad crowd, given what was happening at home for you.**

Modeling this kind of trust in the speaker's goodness is powerful, especially during times when she is buried in self-doubt.

Holding the Reality of the Speaker's Goodness

Think of yourself as trying to communicate the following message to the client (though not necessarily in words): "I'm solidly grounded in the reality of what a good person you are; you can dive into those bad feelings you have toward yourself, because I'll hold on to the truth." *You aren't trying to talk him out of feeling bad about himself*; your job is to create safety for him to feel what he really feels.

This concept means that if the speaker disagrees with a stand you take, don't fight him on it; it isn't your job to get your partner to have the "right" outlook. Your love and your support for his healing processes will be much more effective than your efforts to fix what's "wrong" with his thinking. (In fact, if you keep insisting that he's a good person, the message he'll take from that is, "My partner can't handle hearing how bad I feel about myself." And that we definitely want to avoid.)

Be The Source of Hope

Being an anchor also means that during your partner's turn it's your job to hold the hopefulness. You show through your posture, your facial expression, and the things that you say, that you're optimistic about his life. At times you'll need to hold out hope about the world itself. In other words, *you need to stretch out of your own discouragement while you are in the listening role*. When it's your turn, you can let your own feelings of hopelessness in and work to heal them. But when you're the counselor you're creating safety for your partner to process his despair, and that means you need to stay out of yours.

Two people rarely heal well when they are both feeling deep pain at the same moment. We need to know that someone is on shore, holding tightly to our tether, before we can take on that raging ocean of grief, panic, or lost hope. This is part of why we split time; so that one person can fall apart while the other stands guard.

Reassure Your Partner

The speaker needs to know that she's safe right now. This need can be acute when people are reliving events from their past; old feelings can seem so real that past and present become hard to distinguish. As the listener, you might say things like:

Listener: **What happened back then is completely over now, and it's safe now for you to feel what it was like for you.**

Listener: **I will never put you down the way those people did. No attack is going to happen here.**

Listener: **That was all long ago, and you're safe here with me.**

Listener: **You have the strength now to keep something like that from ever happening again.**

Your partner may also need reassurance that her feelings will not be too much to handle. Encourage her to go ahead and feel whatever's inside her, even if it's scary or overwhelming. Let her know that you'll stay by her and that you aren't worried about her, that you know she'll be fine.

You can help the speaker work through memories that are making the situation in the present feel unsafe, by asking:

Listener: **What feels scary about this session today? What feels like it might happen?**

Another great question for building safety is:

Listener: **What do you need me never to do or say?**

Once you ask this question, of course, you'll need to honor the trust she puts in you by answering.

People feel unsafe because of ways that they were badly hurt or violated, often by people that they trusted. Your goal is to help the speaker feel the difference between the current safety and the past danger she lived with.

Physical Closeness and Aware Touching

Thoughtful, caring, non-invasive touch is one of the greatest promoters of emotional healing. Closeness is essential to effective counseling. When you are in the listener role, sit near the speaker and hold one or both of his hands unless he specifically prefers that you not. The more you work through blocks you have to being physically close to someone in a loving and non-sexual way, the more effective your counseling will become.

Watch for cues from the client that she needs to have you sitting closer, needs you to put your arm around her, or needs to be held. Conversely, be aware of times when she needs more distance from you or needs not to be touched at all. The signals in either direction are there if we pay close attention.

As you develop an ongoing healing partnership with someone, discuss explicitly what kind of closeness feels comfortable and helpful to them when they are the client.

When I say that it's important to work through barriers to physical closeness, I am *not* referring to *your* turn as the speaker; you decide what kind of closeness *if any* is good for you during your turn. For some people, particularly those who've been abused, the healing direction in the short term is toward being *less* physically close to people while they reclaim control over their boundaries.

And even when you're in the listening role, don't engage in touch that you think is unhealthful for you; challenge yourself a little but not too much, and keep listening to your instincts.

The Power of Holding On

When someone begins to cry hard or go into other deep releases, it's often helpful to her to hold onto you tightly. This physical closeness and safety can make it possible for her to pour out stored pain like a collapsing dam. The experience of letting old pain flow out of us is one of the most wonderful aspects of human experience, a profound mixture of pleasure and pain as we feel ourselves healing; and these moments come most commonly when someone is holding us.

What If Physical Touch is Too Triggering for You or Doesn't Feel Right?

Some people's history makes affection feel unsafe or re-injuring for them even when that touch is done thoughtfully and doesn't cross boundaries. If this is true for you, you may need a great deal of healing before physical contact can be a positive experience. It won't help you to rush this process; keep paying close attention to what is good for you. Affection that you aren't ready for will slow your healing, not speed it up.

In the context of splitting time, though, the following question arises: What do you do when you feel uncomfortable providing the kind of affection that the other person needs during her turn? What if, for example, she needs to be held tightly in order to cry hard but you aren't comfortable holding her?

There are two ways to work with this. One solution is to find a healing partner who is in the same boat; people who prefer not to be touched do well to work together.

A second way, which works for a fair number of people, is to make a sharp mental distinction between times when you're receiving support and times when you're giving it. Some people find that they can push through the barriers to physical touch during the other person's turn, but definitely don't want any contact during their own. You can experiment with this approach and see if that's still too triggering.

Above all, *don't continue in physical contact with someone you're co-counseling with if there's anything about that person's energy or intentions that don't feel right to you. If you happen to be misreading them, that's okay; better safe than sorry.*

Don't Soothe Your Partner

In order to avoid triggering, "Don't feel," or "Don't cry," messages that the person has gotten, avoid stroking, rocking, or patting him. If he's in deep feelings keep a hand on him or hold him but *keep your hands still*; you want to help him feel safe enough to continue forward into his feelings, not to distract or soothe him from them.

Ask Lots of Questions

Asking questions is the key way to communicate to the speaker that you care about what he's been through and are eager to learn more. Work steadily on developing your ability to ask questions that show that you:

- are really thinking about what the speaker is saying.

- want to know more about his experience.

- get what his experience has meant to him.

- want to support him to feel his feelings.

Build this skill more and more into your whole life, not just into occasions when you're splitting time with someone. As I covered in detail Chapter 3, asking more and better questions is the key to connectedness among human beings and propels emotional healing.

Counseling With All Parts of Yourself

When you're the listener, your imagination, your intuition, and your heart play big roles. Structure and techniques provide a framework but they don't need to box you in. Ask yourself, "What could I try today that might make the speaker feel how much I care? How might I get through those walls of discouragement? How could I do an end run around my partner's brain and go straight for the heart?"

Creativity can enter in various forms. Someone who was counseling me once created a little puppet out of tissues and drew a face on it, helping me to use laughter as a way to overcome feelings of powerlessness. A man I used to split time with loved to have me make up colorful stories about how things should have happened when he was born. Some people respond well to feeling "mothered," because of ways that adults did not nurture them adequately as children; you create this atmosphere for your client through affection, softening your voice, and taking a caretaking (but not pitying) tone. Some people need to get physical, pounding pillows or a mattress while venting their rage, or pushing against you (with your permission, of course).

As the listener, keep thinking outside the box; imaginative approaches will often touch your partner more deeply than just expressing your support in words.

Love Your Partner

Love may not heal us all by itself, but it's certainly the single greatest stimulator of our healing processes. Connect with the most loving feelings toward the speaker that you can. In PLN we strive to stop being afraid to love each other and to let it show, because we grasp the power of love.

———

There is always more to learn about how to be the most effective anchor for someone's healing. The development of your listening and counseling skills will be a life-long project. When you're finished with this book, I recommend that you read *The Healing Partnership: A Manual for Splitting Time* at PeakLivingNetwork.org; that manual offers extensive guidance and techniques.

Getting the Most from Your Own Turns

The Peak Living Network is not about making small improvements in our lives; We're aiming for transformation, for the building of a whole new life and a new world.

My life own is divided in two; the one I lived until my twenties when I learned how to heal, and the life I have lived since. The two periods are as different as night and day. (My story is in the Appendix.) I know that transformation is possible because I've lived it and seen it in other people.

Set your sights high. Do serious work in your sessions and use your time consciously. Allow time for rest and fun in your turns as well. Take healthy risks in how much you open yourself up. Allow feelings to come in that you're afraid to feel, and release them when you can. You'll get from splitting time what you put into it.

You and Your Healing Partner are a Team

During your turn you and your co-counselor are combining your intelligence and creativity, *thinking together* about how best to help you. Then, during your partner's turn, the two of you are thinking together about how best to help him. It's when we put our heads together that great things start to happen.

Old injuries can get in the way of this teamwork orientation. One obstacle is the internal voice that says, "No one ever really comes through, so it's up to me to take care of myself." This wound can lead us to stay closed off to our partner rather than opening up to his support and ideas. Another barrier is an opposite voice that says, "I'm helpless so my partner needs to figure things out for me, and I'll feel disappointed and irritated if she doesn't." Good sessions happen when we avoid both of these, taking in the other person's support but also thinking well about ourselves and our needs.

Ask for What You Need

Asking other people for what we need is challenging. We may feel embarrassed to ask or to be perceived as "needy." We may be afraid that we'll burden the other person with our requests for help. Sometimes the very fact that we have to ask seems to ruin everything, because a wounded place inside of us feels that if the other person really cared they'd know what we needed and give it without being asked.

Learn to let your co-counselor know how best to assist you. Ask him to sit closer or move farther away from you; ask him to repeat a particular phrase that you feel the need to hear; ask him for reassurance when you're in doubt or feeling bad about yourself.

Similarly, ask him to push you where you need to be pushed. You might say, for example, "I think I'm avoiding feeling certain feelings, so I need you to keep after me." Or you might say, "I get embarrassed when I express anger, so I could use a lot of encouragement about letting out angry feelings."

Advocate for yourself about things you'd prefer that your counselor *not* do. Let her know if parts of what she says throw you off track or trigger you in a way that isn't helpful. Be open to suggestions, but remember that you get to decide what's the best use of your own time.

Living to Heal, Not Just Healing to Live

Healing helps us live better lives, but the opposing current is just as important; *living better lives helps us heal.* The energy needs to move in both directions. This dynamic is widely overlooked and central to making healing a joyous process rather than a struggle. Don't just look to your sessions to improve the quality of your life, look also to your life to improve the quality of your sessions. Your ability to process and discharge emotions depends a lot on what you do *between* sessions.

The remainder of this book is devoted to helping you develop this back-and-forth between energy devoted to healing and energy poured towards taking important steps in your life. Once this feedback loop really gets going for you the sky is the limit. We'll be looking at:

- the importance of living with courage.

- how to improve the clarity of your thinking so that you move toward better decision-making.

- how to set and meet life goals.

- how to improve the way you take care of yourself.

- how to keep drawing upon your healing partner(s), your healing network, and your healing processes.

During your sessions, dive into the depths of how hard things feel to you, your pain and self-doubt and discouragement. But between sessions focus your attention and energy on *living*; pay attention to what you find satisfying or challenging in your current life, remember what a good person you are, take pride in how you've survived. When your inner turmoil tries to demand your attention, see if you can tell it that you'll be setting aside healing time soon—maybe even that same day—and ask it to let you focus on your current life until then.

Breaking out of our limiting patterns doesn't mean that we necessarily try to do *more*. As we heal from old injuries we find that the *quality* of what we do increases, but not always the *quantity*. Remember the need for rest, relaxation, and regeneration. Keep returning to splitting time to get the support you need, processing and releasing the distresses that your courageous actions are bringing up for you.

Giving Up Numbness

Our experiences of trauma and neglect force us to learn how to numb ourselves in order to survive. Beginning in childhood we discover avenues to pain relief: Filling our heads up with distractions, harming ourselves (because physical pain can block out emotional pain), eating sweets (the most easily accessible numbing substance), or staring at video screens.

Thank heaven we learned how to numb ourselves out, or the pain would have killed us. In the present, though, we long to shake free of the limitations that those survival mechanisms have placed around our lives. And in order to heal we have to have access to our feelings. So rather than reaching for that next doughnut or cigarette or cocktail, train yourself to reach out for a hug, or take a few minutes to cry, or call one of your healing partners to split some time. We don't have to keep chasing our feelings away.

Substances and Splitting Time

Substances affect the quality of our attention, and people around us can feel the difference whether they're conscious of it or not. So when you're in the listening role, the more you can be free of alcohol, caffeine, nicotine, and other substances, the more healing power you have to share with the speaker.

I recognize that if you're going insane from needing a cigarette, or you're nodding off because you haven't had your coffee, you're not going to be a great support. But all the more reason to start working to get free from addiction (see Chapter 15).

As I explained earlier, when people laugh, cry, or get the shakes under the influence of a substance *the normal benefits of the inherent releases don't result*; for some reason that we don't fully understand, nothing actually gets released. Psych meds can also get in the way; many people complain that their meds block them from feeling much of a range of emotions. But I've also spoken with people who report having done significant healing work while on a med. Therefore, PLN does not discourage people from using psych meds, but we do support people to cautiously work free from meds when they decide they want to.

Going Deep

The safer you come to feel with your healing partner and the more you work the steps in this book, the greater the likelihood that you will have sessions where profound emotions move through you. You may be surprised at times by the intensity of what you feel and you may even remember events that you had partly or entirely forgotten. These powerful feelings may be accompanied by wild laughter, hysterical crying, or deep trembling.

Or you may be in the counseling role while these things happen for your partner.

The most important thing to understand about these paroxysms is that *this is where the most profound healing of all takes place*. Much of what we've been trained to view as "insane" is actually the healthiest deep discharging of accumulated traumatic pain. *There's nothing to worry about.* I've gone to such places dozens, perhaps hundreds, of times, and people I've been supporting have done so as well.

What the speaker most needs is for the listener to remain confident and relaxed. If you're in the counseling role, keep indicating to the speaker through your words, facial expression, and body posture that you know she is fine and is doing what she needs to do. As long as you remain okay, the speaker will too. You can even smile once in a while, which the speaker will find reassuring.

There is no such thing as crying or laughing too hard. But what about when the client becomes terrified? How do you know if she has gone to a place that's not healthful for her? I examined this question in detail in Chapter 8, and here's a quick recap:

1) Ask her if she feels like she can handle what she's feeling. If she says "yes," let her keep going. Offer her pillows or cushions to hit and encourage her to let her voice loose. Keep a hand on her unless she indicates that she doesn't want you to.

2) She is likely to cycle through fear, sadness, and anger. Support her to ride the waves of emotion and to release whatever she can release.

3) If she gets to the point where she says that she needs it to stop, guide her out of the deep place. You do this by having her take deep breaths and directing her attention to sights, sounds, smells, and other body sensations from the present moment. Ask her questions about light-hearted subjects, including anything she's looking forward to. You can also walk with her around the room or outside around the building to help her attain calm, or try putting on music.

What if quite a while goes by trying these techniques and she still can't shake the terror? (In over three decades of splitting time with people I've never seen this happen, but it could.) Simply ask her if she wants you to call for professional help. Don't call for help without her permission, though, unless she is threatening to hurt herself or hurt someone else.

Deep feelings rarely become unmanageable as long as the person is being assisted to discharge the emotions; many mental health crises are caused by the surrounding people lacking understanding of the inherent releases.

We all need to overcome our fears of going to deep places and of witnessing each other doing so. A little weepy cry hardly heals anything, but a hysterical sobbing "flip out" heals a ton.

Make Your Healing a Priority

Modern life has become highly scheduled and pressured. In this mad rush it's easy for our health and happiness to end up at the bottom of the priority list. When I tell people that they should get a two-hour co-counseling session once a week with additional short phone sessions in between, they look at me like I'm asking the impossible. But when splitting time is going well, the extra energy and clarity that grow from your sessions will give you those two hours back and a lot more besides.

If full-length sessions are truly impossible for you—as is true for some parents, for example—then go for frequency. Build relationships with three or four different people to co-counsel with on the phone, and see if you can split ten or fifteen minutes with one of them every day. Squeeze in an in-person session whenever you can even if you each only get half-hour turns.

Your healing is a priority and you deserve that time. Notice when you're falling into putting it last, and promote it back toward the top.

If you have children, time is harder to find. But your children benefit when you get good chunks of time each week to soak up love and support and do the emotional processing you need. They end up with a parent who is more present, more patient, and more affectionate.

Phone Time

Develop a good number of different people you can call for a quick session on the phone. You could call:

- your regular healing partner if you have one.

- someone you met at a local PLN Open Support Meeting or in a book group for *The Joyous Recovery.*

- a friend to whom you've explained the basics of splitting time.

You won't usually do your deepest work in a quick phone session, but a few minutes of attending to your feelings and absorbing love and support from the listener can have a surprising impact on your day. Those few minutes also lay groundwork for going deep on a day when you have a longer session.

Reach out even—or especially—when it's hard to do. Those moments when you feel like you're in no shape to talk to anyone are exactly when you most need to be reminded that you're unconditionally loved. Pick up the phone and make that call!

Nurture and Treasure Your Healing Partner

The better relationship you build with the person or people you split time with the more you'll be able to use your turns to do deep work. Don't cancel sessions except for an emergency. Bring your full love and attention. Work hard at your co-counseling relationship and stick with it through hard times. If you decide you need to stop splitting time with a certain partner (for logistical reasons or because it's no longer working for you), end the relationship in a loving way, appreciating your partner for who they are and for what they've offered you.

"Report Backs"

Section V of *The Healing Partnership* (on the PLN website) includes a section called, "Report Backs and Supervision." You'll find step-by-step guidelines for strengthening your healing partnership by doing a structured evaluation (with a third person's support) of how your sessions are going. This process gives a lovely boost to a healing partnership and I encourage you to use it.

The Goal is Fulfillment

A life in which you're healing becomes satisfying, meaningful, and fulfilling. It doesn't necessarily get easier; in some ways it may become more challenging. But you find yourself ready to take those challenges on and they start to seem worth it. You approach days with anticipation rather than with dread. You feel more engaged with life, more involved in what's happening, more connected to people.

The successful path to healing is a turbulent one; in the words of the *Tao Te Ching*, "The easy way seems hard." If you're looking for superficial happiness and comfort, you're not likely to find it here. But if you desire a life of purpose and connection and satisfaction, and one where you feel like *a well person*, it's here for you.

And this is what we are most longing for: love, interdependence, and meaning. Sure, we'd like to be happy as much of the time as possible, and we'll keep reaching for that; but that's less urgent than feeling *fulfilled and accompanied*. What really feels good is when we're able to look back several months, or a year, or longer, and feel warm inside about where it's all going. *That* is the joyous recovery.

Have an Impact on Your World

One of the mistakes that run rampant is the notion: "I have to get my own self together before I can be any help to anyone else." The only people this is true for are those who've been burdened for years with having to take care of others in a way that has left no room for their own needs. And even for those people it isn't that they're "too messed up" to help others; it's that they desperately need and deserve a break from caretaking.

You can make a difference in the world right now. Don't view it as a burden; take an opposite view, that having an impact is your birthright. Every human being wants to know that they make a contribution to their community, one that is noticed and valued.

Deciding that we'll heal now and change the world later actually slows our healing down. Some of our deepest wounds come from times when awful things were happening around us and we couldn't do anything about it. Other deep wounds come from ways that we were made to feel unimportant, like we had nothing to offer. We counteract these wounds by declaring our value in the world and putting it into action.

Key Points to Remember:

- You can learn the fundamental skills you need to facilitate another person's deep healing.

- As both members of a healing partnership sharpen their skills, the work you are doing together goes deeper and deeper.

- We heal much better when we're involved in helping others to heal, and help others much better when we're involved in our own healing. The two together is what works well.

- Love the people you do your healing work with and take in the love that they give you.

- Start reaching now for the new life that's possible for you.

Chapter Twelve

The Peak Living Network

Suppose that you spent a significant chunk of time each week around people who were dedicated to their own healing. And they didn't just talk about healing; they were really moving, and you could feel it happening. Can you picture how that would propel your own recovery? Can you picture yourself tapping into the hopefulness, the energy, the successes, and the courage that you'd be hearing about from other people's lives?

You can experience these kinds of surroundings by being part of a healing network. Participants in a healing network get to know each other better and better over time, share their triumphs, come through for each other in hard times, and benefit from learning about what's working for other people.

Here's a picture of how different life can be:

It's Monday morning. Megan has breakfast and then she calls Grant, a man she knows from her local PLN group. She asks him, "Do you have time to split fifteen minutes with me?" He does. Megan gets a turn to talk about why she's feeling down-hearted as she heads into her work week. She feels better from getting Grant's support and encouragement. Grant also takes a turn, which actually helps both of them; it helps Grant because of the support he receives, and it helps Megan because listening to Grant's feelings deepens her sense of connection to him. She heads out into her day feeling like she's carrying a piece of Grant with her, giving her strength.

On Tuesday night, Megan meets with another person she has clicked with through PLN, Corinne; they have started to meet weekly to split time in person. They meet for nearly two hours, each taking 50-minute turns. Megan processes a bunch of what's been going on inside her, including several minutes when something shakes loose inside of her and she cries hard. She feels energized and clear-headed after the session.

At lunch time on Friday, Megan goes to the Open Support Meeting for her local PLN network. Megan and Grant are both there that week, along with some other people whom she's been looking forward to seeing. People at the meeting are warm and kind with each other, and there are lots of hugs when the meeting breaks up. There are also a couple of new people at the meeting, who receive warm welcomes and are encouraged to keep coming. Megan gets to talking with one of them for a few minutes after the meeting, a woman named Sabina, and comes away with a very positive impression of her. They exchange phone numbers

Sabina calls Megan a couple of days later and asks if she could get a little support about the awkwardness of coming to the support group for the first time. Megan listens to Sabina for five minutes and gives her reassurance and support. Then Megan takes a turn, and in this way Sabina learns a little about the process of splitting time.

The following Thursday evening, Megan's PLN women's group gathers for its monthly meeting. This event is something like an Open Support Meeting but with some differences; it's just for women, it's led by the same person each month, and people who come to it are asked to attend regularly and not just drop in. But it still follows PLN principles.

Megan loves the healing power of a women-only group, and the extra safety she feels to work on ways she has felt affected by sexism over the past month, especially at work. She also enjoys being at a meeting that's run by an experienced leader, a woman named Kelly who agreed to take on the regular facilitating of the women's group. Corinne is there as well.

On this Friday Megan decides not to go to her usual Open Support Meeting since she had her women's group the night before and needs the time to run errands.

On Sunday, Megan gets a call from Corinne, telling her that Grant's mother has just passed away. Corinne and another person from their PLN network, Justin, are heading to Grant's house to be there for him, and Grant asked Corinne to see if Megan could come too. Megan says yes and meets up with everyone half an hour later at Grant's house. Megan and Justin don't know each other well but she's heard from Grant that he and Justin have been doing co-counseling sessions together so she has an instant sense of Justin as an ally.

They all stay at Grant's house for two or three hours, supporting him while he makes phone calls, packs his bags, and breaks frequently into tears. A friend of Grant's who isn't part of the healing network also comes over and adds his support and presence, and that friend then drives Grant to the airport.

A week or so later Megan decides to catch up on blog posts on the PLN website, reading an interesting article about the emotional impact of job loss and unemployment. She writes a long comment to the post, based on an experience she went through a few years ago. An online dialogue ensues over the next several days, with people sharing what they've been through when they've lost jobs and swapping ideas about how to best support each other at such times. One person writes about the need to create a society where people aren't just dumped from their jobs, and various people share their thoughts on that theme.

All of the online communicating is done with kindness and respect, even when people disagree with what someone else wrote;

this gentle "we're all here to care about each other" tone is expected and required on all PLN forums.

The next week Corinne is away, and Megan doesn't want to miss having a full-length session. Megan decides to give Sabina a try, and they meet to split time. They end up really hitting it off. She encourages Sabina to join the women's group.

A few Saturdays later, it's time for the four-times-a-year gatherings that happen in Megan's local PLN network. You might call the gathering a mini-workshop. From 1:00-5:00 in the afternoon, everyone from the network who can make it comes together. Some of the time is spent in the whole group, hearing brief news from people's lives and listening to a talk on healing techniques that someone volunteered to give. People break into twos for mini-sessions a couple of times during all this, and Megan gets to connect with some people she doesn't see very often.

Then there's a big group game, with lots of laughter.

Then people break up into small groups for about an hour to pursue specific topic areas; at this season's gathering the groups are offered on such topics as combating chronic health problems, helping children cope with the educational system, and caring for elderly parents. Megan decides to attend a group for people who want to pursue a new direction in their work lives. She gets support there and ideas for next steps toward a job change.

Megan leaves this gathering so energized that she decides to volunteer for a half-year stint on the Planning Committee of her healing network. That committee does things like plan the next season's local gathering, recruit people to lead more monthly support groups, plan an evening on improving counseling skills (which they try to offer a few times per year), and connect with the national Peak Living Network steering committee.

Three months later, Megan decides to drive several hours to participate in a large weekend PLN gathering that is drawing people from all around her part of the country. This workshop is led by a certified PLN teacher, and costs a few hundred dollars to attend, but Megan can swing it because it's the only activity related to her healing network that she has spent any money on that year(!); most of the time the network functions through people trading attention, not by trading money.

The weekend retreat leaves Megan feeling connected to the Peak Living Network as a national and global movement—as a network of networks, you might say—that goes way beyond her own local network. She loves many of the people she meets and her healing is launched forward by feeling connected to so many people living by the same principles. Together, they're all discovering their power to make a difference.

———————

There's only so far we can get when we're trying to heal by ourselves, or with only one or two people—a therapist, for example—to help us. We need *a whole army behind us*, we need *those people to be healing too*, and we need *to be hearing about their healing*.

Growth sprouts from many directions for a person who gets involved with the Peak Living Network:

1) *Being able to connect quickly to people you didn't know before.* This unusually rapid connection is made possible by the fact that everyone has agreed to the PLN Statement of Principles. That means right from the start you can assume the other person:

- believes in kindness and in listening well.

- believes in respect and equality for all human beings.

- believes in letting people laugh and cry as much as they need to.

- believes that we can make the world a better place.

- believes that we're all smart and capable.

That's a huge amount of instant common ground.

2) *Having access to people to split time with, including people who keep working on improving their listening and counseling skills.* It's like having a team of therapists instead of one. Plus you can almost always reach one of them by phone. Plus when things are really hard one of them comes over to your home.

3) *Sharing information about successful healing strategies and approaches to counseling each other well.* Through PLN literature, online forums, presentations at gatherings, and resources we share with each other, participants in PLN are constantly learning more and drawing on the experience of people from all different backgrounds.

4) *Attending gatherings of various lengths, from a few hours to a few days, where people come together to experience the power of group support—and to have fun together—with other people whose lives are unfolding.* Group events devoted to healing and following the Peak Living Network approach have a potent impact.

Megan's story illustrates the key elements of what a vibrant healing network has to offer:

- people to split time with (co-counseling sessions)
- open support groups
- support groups on specific themes or for specific constituencies (especially oppressed groups)
- gatherings for an entire local network
- gatherings that are regional or national

- training classes and workshops on counseling skills, led by a certified PLN teacher

- training classes and workshops to become a certified PLN teacher

Sessions and support groups are all free, and most other gatherings charge only enough to cover expenses (such as room rental). The only exception is certain training classes and workshops that may charge fees if they're led by a certified PLN teacher; but even then the fees are kept low and allowances are made for people with fewer economic resources to be able to participate. And no one has to participate in *any* paid activities in order to be part of the network.

The Larger Peak Living Network

The central PLN organization offers PLN books and other literature, training to become a certified PLN teacher, and a range of supports to individuals working on creating, building, and strengthening local networks. We are here to support your leadership and are happy to consult with you—at no charge—on your efforts to work locally.

A tremendous amount of information is available at PeakLivingNetwork.org:

- the PLN Statement of Principles

- guidelines and suggestions for creating a local network

- contact information for areas that already have an established network

- free literature, including a complete manual for splitting time called *The Healing Partnership*

- ordering information for PLN books

- a calendar of upcoming PLN trainings

- the PLN online forum, with conversations you can join on various topics

How to Plug In

If your area already has a local network, you can find the contact person at PeakLivingNetwork.org under "Local Groups." That person can help you find healing partners, let you know what support groups exist, and tell you how you can help build the network. In that same section of the website you'll find information about how to create a local group if none exists for your area.

If you're looking for people to split time with and there's no contact person yet for your area, go to the PLN website and click on "Find Healing Partners." As soon as you find even one other person who lives near you, that's the beginning of a local network. In the mean time, keep reading this book and the materials on the website.

The mission of the Peak Living Network is to dramatically increase *everyone's* access to the necessary resources for emotional healing. We want your involvement. Please join us!

Key Point to Remember:

- Your success and progress in healing emotionally will jump to a new level when you become part of a healing network based on mutual support. You can find out more at PeakLivingNetwork.org.

Part Three

Taking Our Lives Back

Chapter Thirteen

Reclaiming Personal Power

Consider the following energizing healing cycle:

We take powerful action in the world ⋯→

Our actions, and the world's reactions to what we do, stir feelings inside us ⋯→

We set aside time for healing, including processing and releasing our painful feelings, getting support, and getting rest ⋯→

We reflect, learn, and strategize ⋯→

We take renewed powerful action in the world

You can get this powerful cycle moving, as we will see.

We are now going to examine power in its constructive forms: the power to take charge of your life, the power to create, the power to cooperate, the power to liberate.

A few opening points about personal power:

- We have the right to *full say* over *all* the decisions that affect us and those we care about. No one's say should be any greater than anyone else's. When our full say is taken away our power erodes, and we end up having to fight hard to restore our rights.

- We have the power to *create*. Your creative power may be as a builder, a grower of food, a parent, a musician, a community organizer, a cook, a potter, a healer. These people are creating beautiful meals, creating beautiful surroundings, creating beautiful social processes, creating wellness. (And in a healthy world all of these people interact with the natural world to keep humans and the natural realm in harmony.)

- We have the power to *influence*. Our perspectives are important to other people of all ages. We each contribute to the growth of common understandings. We grow and change from the things we learn from those around us, and we are simultaneously all teachers.

- We have the power to *cooperate*. Instead of getting infected by the modern disease of seeking power *over* other people, we want to develop our power with each other, working together to pursue common goals and make beautiful things happen. We want to create processes in which everyone's contribution is valued and what we build benefits everyone.

- We have the power to *defend ourselves and those we love*. This power has been taken from many of us by systems of oppression that punish people for defending themselves. We can reclaim this power of self-defense individually and collectively.

- We have the power to *set right what is wrong in the world around us*. It's not our fault that we've come to feel powerless; we developed those feelings from experiences in which there truly was nothing we could do about injustices around us. But powerlessness is not the deep truth about us; we can find ways to take back our power and set things right. The wish to do so is among our deepest cravings.

Overcoming Blocks to Acting Powerfully

Assuming That We're Powerless

We tend to go through life assuming that there's little we can do to improve most things that bother us; this view is so deeply rooted that we don't notice we harbor it. We learn to cast our eyes down and trudge through life while frustrations and resentments accumulate.

The roots of this outlook are in early experiences when we, or people we loved, were being wronged, and we were too small, isolated, and inexperienced to do anything about it. *These experiences of powerlessness are among our deepest hurts.*[1] After these kinds of events happen enough times, powerlessness comes to feel like an inevitable aspect of life.

Today, begin noticing situations in which you doubt that you can significantly influence events around you. Ask yourself, "Is it true that there's nothing I can do, or are those just feelings left over from old injuries? What could I attempt that might make a difference?"

Here's an example: You're standing in line in a store, and nearby a mother is being mean to her children. You feel bad

---

[1] "The essence of trauma is helplessness" - Dr. Joyanna Silberg, *The Child Survivor*

for them, but you think, "If I say anything she'll rage at me, and that will upset her kids even more." Instead of giving up, though, you try to catch her kids' eyes. You use the eye contact to send them a smile, conveying the message that you can see she's being hard on them.

This small action is more important than you may realize. Your compassionate eye contact may be a voice in the wilderness for those children. Seeing that someone notices and cares about what's happening can sustain kids for days after. In fact, I can remember as a child how much strength I absorbed from my interactions with a loving friend of my mother's whom I saw once every *few years*. I also remember the boosts I would get from a neighbor who stopped to talk to me for a few minutes, an uncle who invited me to go for a walk with him, a stranger who joked with me in a parking lot.

Meanwhile, your small action carries a message back to you that says, "This is the type of person I want to be, this is who I truly am." You're getting a little taste of your own power which will lead you to bigger actions in the future.

Start shifting your outlook toward the assumption that you can make a difference, that you can set right what is wrong. And the times when you find yourself in a situation where you truly can't think of anything to try, tell yourself, "I haven't figured this one out yet," rather than, "That's just the way life is."

Feeling That It's None of Our Business

Bullies of all kinds, whether at school, on the street, or at home, react to challengers by saying, "Mind your own business—this has nothing to do with you!" But it *always* has to do with you. Any time a person, an animal, or the natural environment is being harmed, *it's your business.* Until very recent times in human history, people have considered it their responsibility to ensure that *everyone* was well, and that nature was cared for.

People who abuse their power—whether owners of a workplace, tyrants in the home, or police on the street—try to keep their targets isolated by saying that "bystanders" have no right to get involved. In response, we need to say loudly and proudly, "It's my business because we're all human beings!"

Fear of Disapproval

Whenever we draw attention to things that aren't right, we create discomfort in others. And they tend to react by blaming the messenger. We see this dynamic in families with an alcoholic or abusive parent; when one child dares to name the problem, the rest of the family pours energy into criticizing and isolating the child who spoke the truth. We see similar patterns in other groups and organizations.

Here are ways through this trap:

- Before raising an issue, build allies; don't go it alone if you can avoid it. When other people are willing to take a stand with you, it's harder for the group to scapegoat you.

- Spend some time, either in journal writing or a co-counseling session, processing your earlier experiences of being targeted or blamed after you challenged a wrong. This step helps you prepare for the current challenge.

- If you receive a "blame the messenger" response, name it aloud while remaining calm and educational in your tone. You might try saying, "I sense that you're mad at me for bringing up this difficult subject. See if you can just take in what I'm saying." And don't give up, even if you have to raise the issue over and over again.

Not Being Sure You Deserve Better

It's hard to take back your power if you're feeling like you don't know enough, or haven't worked hard enough, or haven't been self-sacrificing enough. But *everybody* deserves to be treated well and have a good life. Plus, when your life improves, the good results spread to others.[2]

Some adults dismiss children's upset feelings with callous expressions like, "Life is hard" or "The world isn't fair." Children's emotions are just as valid as those of adults, and they are *right* to expect a world that's fair. We want them to go through life fighting for what's right, don't we? So help them process their frustrations and sadnesses, support them to cry as much as they need to, and then strategize with them about ways to gather support and act powerfully.

Risk of Retaliation

Perhaps the greatest obstacle to reclaiming power is the danger that someone will get you back for it. Particularly for people from oppressed groups, telling someone, "Go out there and take your power back!" could be a prescription for getting them badly hurt.

---

[2] What about people who improve their lives through selfish acts? The answer is they don't. Though they may act triumphant, they are secretly miserable. Selfishness is a dead end.

So fighting back requires that we balance these questions:

"How much of my fear is based on real dangers, and how much of it is based on old injuries?"

"How can I lessen my risk by allying with other people?"

*"Has it become time to stand up for my rights even if I do pay a price? What are the costs of **not** trying to reclaim my power?"*

"How will my choices about fighting back affect my children and others around me?"

These are hard questions. If anyone claims they know the answers for you, or acts dismissive when you discuss the thorniness of these decisions, they're out of line. Let's support each other to grapple with these questions.

In Chapter 19, I talk about the process of joining together with other people to take collective power. We are usually safer when we take organized social action than when we fight on our own.

"What Gives Me the Right to Decide What Needs to Be Done?"

It's easy to feel as though you need someone's authorization before you move decisively in the world. *But if no one else is doing what needs to be done, then you're exactly the right person to do it.* Don't wait for permission.

Taking Leadership

We *all* can be leaders, and need to be. See yourself as a leader, or at least as a leader-in-training. I'm not saying we should lead all the time; we have our areas of strength, clarity, and passion. I lead weekend retreats because I'm good at it and love doing it. But I won't volunteer to manage my baseball team because I don't have the right skills and don't feel called to it. Find the particular areas where your leadership can blossom.

Leadership Is Not About Deciding *For* People

Leadership gets mistakenly confused with ruling or dictating. Good leaders don't make decisions for others; they empower others to make plans and take action. They are constantly in dialogue with the people they're leading, collecting perspectives and information in order to:

- figure out a good course of action and propose it to the group.
- modify the proposal, bringing in elements of each person's best thinking.
- work with the group until a course is mapped out that everyone feels okay about.

There are additional roles that a leader takes on from time to time:

- noticing when certain people are not being heard or are being misunderstood and points that out
- taking actions that require courage, such as intervening when someone is mistreated or endangered
- working to gain knowledge or skill in a specific area so that others might benefit from those abilities
- making quick decisions in an emergency, just until the next opportunity to gather for group decision-making

- teaching others

Teaching is a type of leadership. And you have important things to teach other people; everyone does.

Being a parent is the essence of leadership. If you're raising children you're developing leadership skills every day that you can translate to other areas of life.

Start thinking of yourself as a leader. Consider ways to strengthen, expand, and humanize your leadership, deepening your connections to people as you go.

What Does "Full Say" Look Like?

Adult humans have the right to full and equal say over *all* decisions that affect their lives and those they care about. Your opinions and preferences are as important as anyone's. Children have a right to substantial say, and that right should grow steadily toward equality as they approach adulthood.

But in modern society it's considered acceptable for a tiny percentage of the population to make all the key decisions. Our lives are mostly determined in corporate boardrooms and government hallways. If you dare suggest that we have the right to equal say where we work, you'll be labeled a socialist. Many of us have a scary tyrant even within our own homes. Major realms of life have been taken over by smiling, successful bullies.

We need to start preparing ourselves to take it all back. Take pride in your rebelliousness; don't let the bosses make you ashamed of it. Focus on your true rights, including the full say you deserve at home, at work, and in the halls of power. Think of yourself as someone who has come to reclaim what belongs to you and to your people.

"I'm Scared to Act Powerfully Even When There's No Danger"

Many of us struggle with a vague, looming sense that if we make big changes or take courageous steps, something bad will happen. But when we go ahead and take the leap, the results are usually positive. At the same time, we don't make lasting change by lurching blindly forward through our terror. What works over time is:

- journal writing to prepare yourself to take a scary step

- spending time in co-counseling sessions feeling your fear and anxiety about taking the brave action ahead, and drawing on your releases (especially laughter)

- finding ways to gather more support than you've had before, including if possible being accompanied by a supportive person right when you take the scary step

- getting support *after* taking the step, including more journal writing, co-counseling time, and support from friends

The last piece is the one most commonly missing. What makes courageous effort sustainable is the support and processing we draw upon *after* taking the initiative.

Living from Choice

Some of the bullies we have to stand up to are inside of our own heads. We have voices, left there by old wounds, telling us that we're not smart enough, we'll never get it right, we have to give up.

One way to forcefully challenge these voices is to *argue*

with them out loud. You can do this in a co-counseling session or by yourself; put power and anger in your voice and yell back at those negative messages:

"Shut up!"

"Yes I can!"

"You don't know what you're talking about!"

"I'll be able to handle it just fine!"

We can also yell positive messages at ourselves. I'm an athlete, and if you watched me lifting weights or sprinting across a field you might hear me shouting, "Come on!" or "You can totally do this!" or "Yes! Way to go!"

Life becomes more satisfying when we live *from choice* rather than from habit, fear, or unconscious limitations. Our unhealed emotional wounds push us away from making conscious decisions and into:

- unthinking behavior.

- behavior driven by a sense that this what we "must" do.

- behavioral habits that feed our exaggerated need for comfort (a need that itself results from our wounds).

- behavior rooted in the belief that we're not as capable as we really are.

As you go through your day, start to examine the things that you do. But avoid the judgmental lens of good vs. bad and right vs. wrong; instead, ask yourself whether you are choosing your actions. "Is this really what I want to be doing? Is some unseen force driving me to do this? Am I really as restricted as I feel right now, or do I have other options?"

I know a man who served 14 years in jail. Huge aspects

of Juan's life were entirely beyond his control in prison, including painful injustices that he couldn't prevent; a person can't "live from choice" in a brutal prison system. But in the short time since Juan was released, he has built a successful business *run cooperatively by the people who work in it*. His work is expressing values that are the opposite of the toxic jail environment—and some of his co-workers are former prisoners themselves.

It's important not to blame yourself for what you can't do, or for what you can't do *yet*. But be on the constant lookout for ways to expand what you *can* do. Our ability to live from choice can grow and grow.

Acting From Our Deep Wisdom

We don't have to be pushed around by our leftover feelings from past wounds. And neither do we have to be pushed around by cold hard logic; logic is a tool, not a guide. There is a place inside each of us that's deeper than thought or feeling, deeper even than intuition. It is our wisdom: the place in our heart of hearts where we know what is true. Our actions should spring from this deep well. Every so often take a deep breath, close your eyes for a moment, and ask yourself, "Are my actions lining up with what I truly know is right? If not, what do I need to do differently?"

Reclaiming Your Boundaries

It is your right to decide who touches you, whom you open up to about personal matters, and who knows the details of your life. But as is true for most people, you've probably encountered individuals who think they have the right to put their hands on you whether you like it or not. Similarly, they may pressure you to talk about private issues that you don't wish to share. *You don't owe pieces of yourself to anyone;* not even your closest friends and relatives, not even your own parents.

At the same time, you don't want to be unconsciously shutting people out that you'd would actually like to be close to.

Start to reflect on your boundaries. Notice interactions that leave you feeling trampled emotionally or physically; and notice especially any individuals that make you feel that way repeatedly. Be aware also of people you're keeping at a distance that you would actually prefer to be closer to. You can learn more in the article "Understanding and Maintaining Boundaries" at PeakLivingNetwork.org.

Key Points to Remember:

- Each of us is naturally a powerful individual.

- Past experiences of powerlessness leave scars that cause us to underestimate our capabilities.

- We have the right to take our power back, and with the right support we can do so.

- Reclaiming power supports our healing, and our healing supports the reclaiming of our power. The two feed each other.

- You have skills, abilities, and insights that the world urgently needs.

Chapter Fourteen

Setting and Meeting Goals

Our next task is to set a life course and learn how to stay on it. Emotional healing moves faster when we aim ourselves toward our deepest values and desires.

Let's explore three concepts in preparation for this work:

1) *Responsibility* and *blame* are two different things. When they get mixed together in our minds, they produce a tenacious glue that keeps us stuck. *Blame* is about who caused a problem; *responsibility* is about who's going to fix it.

Ideally these two things would indeed go together; the people who make the messes should be the ones to clean them up. But in practice that's often not what happens.

Consider an example: An abusive man leaves psychological scars in the children who grow up witnessing his degradation of their mother. He is 100% to blame for the harm he has done. Tragically, though, society lets him get way with ignoring the damage. So who will help those kids get emotionally well?

Mom is absolutely not to blame. But the reality is that she's stuck with the responsibility for helping her kids heal. If we find ourselves supporting a mother in that position, we don't want to ever forget that none of what the abuser did is her fault. At the same time, we have to help her shoulder the burden that's been unfairly dumped on her, because no one else is going to handle it for her.

Take the same outlook on yourself. You didn't cause your own emotional injuries, especially not the ones you endured as a child. You're not to blame when your life feels stuck, or lonesome, or lacking in purpose. But at the same time, nobody else is going to take charge of your healing. It has fallen to you and there's no use pretending otherwise.

You may know someone who keeps waiting for the day when some person (such as the amazing partner they're going to find), or some force (such as God), or some stroke of luck (such as winning the lottery) will take care of everything. And of course it never happens.

Blame won't lead to progress; the more you berate yourself like a nasty sports coach, the thicker the obstacles become. But at the same time, the key agent is *you*. How do you accept that reality without dumping on yourself? The answer is to separate responsibility from blame.

2) Recognizing that the responsibility is yours is *not* the same as saying, "It's all up to you."

Modern life has become individualistic, so that any time a new responsibility drops in our laps we get a sinking feeling of being left alone with it. That's why we become avoidant. But we deserve—and can build—a solid team behind us for each of life's undertakings, for everything from caring for elderly parents to cleaning up the neighborhood.

Avoid the trap of thinking that you shouldn't need help or don't deserve it. *Everyone loves to help people who use help well and who express appreciation.* In fact, people don't even mind helping you with a problem that you created yourself—as long as you don't keep doing it over and over. Find help, use it well, and everyone will be happy.

3) Avoid taking on *additional responsibilities* without accumulating *additional resources.*

No one is an unlimited fountain of energy, time, hopefulness, generosity, and listening. We can all get depleted. For us to have healthy, life-affirming energy flowing from us, energy has to be going *into* us at the same time.

Here are some examples of things that refuel us:

Some Key Resources

- Sleep and other forms of rest, including periods of being awake but quiet

- Warm, nutritious, enjoyable food

- Enjoyable and healthful exercise and time outdoors

- Love, kindness, people who are happy to see us

- Physical affection

- Meaningful work (which isn't necessarily our paid work, though ideally it would be)

- Ideas and information that stimulate our minds and help us figure out good courses of action

- Concrete assistance—actual help with doing what has to be done

- Emotional support and other crucial but intangible assistance

- Financial support

- Help with planning

I want to underline the last item; planning is a lot of work. To run a household, for example, you have to plan meals, juggle everyone's schedules, plan birthday presents and parties for the kids, prepare for the key holidays, stay on budget, and so much more. This vast planning work (done mostly by women) rarely gets recognized.

Now, let's suppose you're considering taking on a new responsibility, such as:

- expanding your work hours, starting a new business, or taking on a volunteer job.

- having a child (or another child).

- taking on the care of an elderly relative.

- buying a house, property, boat, or anything else that requires maintenance.

- enrolling your child in an activity that requires parental involvement.

- starting a degree program.

Get in the habit of asking yourself, "If I undertake this, where will my additional fuel come from? What items—from the resource box above—are going to grow bigger in my life, and how?" Avoid taking on a new load until you figure out what will fuel you; *more responsibility needs to come with more resource.*

The Nuts and Bolts of Goal Work

How often should I do this? I recommend engaging in the goal-work process once every three months, bringing fresh thinking to each season.

Do I need a partner for this work? No, but it helps. If you don't have someone to split time with, go to Peak-LivingNetwork.org and click on "Find Healing Partners." You'll be able to specify that you're looking for a goal-work partner.

How much time will it take? You can make or update a workable plan in about 60-75 minutes. You can shorten the face-to-face time with a partner by doing parts of the work ahead on your own.

Step 1: Create the Categories

To begin, you need paper. It could be a journal or notebook but bigger is better, such as flip-chart sheets or butcher paper. If you use regular sized paper, you'll want a separate sheet for each of the eight categories we'll be exploring. If you're working on a large sheet, make a chart like the one on page 199.

Close relationships: This section is about your closest people. Include goals about meeting new people or propelling existing relationships to a higher level.
   Some examples of goals you might set in this category:

- ways to deepen your relationships

- specific activities you'd like to share with close friends or relatives (such as, "I want to finally plan that trip with my sister that we keep saying we'll do 'some day'")

- people you haven't gotten close to yet but would like to reach out to

You might also include goals regarding your challenges in close relationships, such as:

	3 Months	1 Year	5 Years
Close Relationships			
Health			
Work			
Interests & Hobbies			
Affecting the World			
Emotional Healing			
Children & Other Relatives			
Deep Connection			

- "I want to be able to argue with friends without losing my temper so fast."
- "I want to watch television less and spend more time hanging out with friends."

Health: Here you might address such issues as:

- goals for exercise and healthful eating
- healthcare steps to take, such as seeing a doctor, acupuncturist, or herbalist
- meditation, stretching, yoga, and other strategies for calming anxiety and increasing energy
- engaging more in physical activities that you find pleasurable, such as sitting in the sun, trading massages, soaking in a bath, or going swimming

Work: This realm addresses the primary ways you invest your time and energy, whether paid or unpaid, including homemaking and caring for relatives. Some examples include:

- specific things you'd like to accomplish
- ways to improve your happiness or satisfaction at work, including reducing stress
- goals for organizing employees where you work, such as union-building
- efforts to find a new job or to get education in that direction

Interests: The question to explore here is, "Where does my heart most lie? What is my passion?" You may love collecting rocks, quilting, playing fantasy baseball, or running for city council. *Make sure not to let the years go by without getting to the things that matter most to you.* Check in with yourself about your deepest desires and dreams, and align your goals with them.

Affecting the world: This category concerns our goals for making a difference in our community and beyond; fighting injustice, organizing people to have more of a voice, helping people in need. (See Chapters 18 and 19.) Goals you might have include:

- joining your neighborhood association or creating one

- getting involved with social justice efforts through your church

- finding a local chapter of an organization that inspires you, such as Black Lives Matter or Mothers Out Front, or starting one

Emotional Healing: Our healing work has an unfortunate tendency to fall to the bottom of the priority list. Consider setting goals regarding:

- how often you write in your journal

- carving out time for co-counseling

- walking in nature or visiting the park

- making time to listen to music, read inspiring poems, or have a good cry

Children and other relatives: Our relationships with our children and other relatives have a special quality. Some examples of goals include:

- strategies to get more support regarding your parenting

- ways to reach out to relatives
- efforts to repair rifts or drifts that have occurred over the years
- planning a family gathering

Deep connection: This realms involves a set of widening circles. We begin with our sense of connection to all people, then to all living things, then to everything that exists. (For example, I feel a connection to the beauty of rock that began when I was a young boy wielding a rock hammer.) Most of us feel something special when we reach the top of a mountain and sit quietly with the expansive view. Goals in this area might include:

- spending time in nature
- finding a spiritual community or deepening your involvement with your current one
- developing a meditation or prayer practice
- finding opportunities to experience quiet
- doing group activities that deepen your sense of connection

Step 2: Set Goals In Three Time Frames

For each of these categories, set goals in three time frames:

- What I would like to see happen by a month from now?
- What I would like to see happen by a year from now?
- What I would like to see happen by five years from now?

At this point it's fine to set goals that are a stretch; avoid limiting yourself to only what seems realistic today. On the other hand, you can get discouraged if your goals feel nearly impossible. Push the bounds of what you think you might accomplish but not so far as to make your goals feel absurd.

Write down as many or as few ideas for each time frame as come to mind, then move to the next category.

If you're working with a goal-work partner, you'll find immediate power just in sharing the fact that these things matter to you. We so often talk the least about the things that are the most important to us.

Step 3: Set Out Tasks

Now you can start thinking about what's realistic. Looking at your one-year or five-year goals, for example, ask yourself, "What would be the first action I could take, however small, in the right direction?" It's okay if it's a tiny step. If you have big exercise goals your first task might be to go for one five-minute walk; if you want to pursue a Ph.D., you might begin with a single phone call to inquire about a program.

The key point at this step is to *set yourself up for success*. Choose tasks for the first week that you're confident you can accomplish. Break your goal down into pieces, choosing about two to five steps to take during the next few months. Set rough targets for when you'd like to get each task done. Then continue this process for each of your goals.

Little steps can have a surprisingly large impact on your momentum, building your confidence and hopefulness. The more you feel like someone in motion, rather than someone who is stuck, the more it will become a reality.

Step 4: Reflect On Obstacles And Strategize

Now that you've laid out some intermediate action, the next question is:

"What is likely to get in my way? Which forces, internal and external, are most likely to stall me?"

Some of the obstacles that can surface include:

- "I'm afraid of disappointment. If I don't try, then I won't get my hopes dashed. It feels safer to stay stuck."

- "My partner has subtly negative reactions when s/he senses that I am getting stronger and taking charge of my life."

- "I feel selfish when I make time for pursuing my desires and goals."

- "I have trouble breaking habits that aren't good for me, and those patterns consume my time and energy."

- "I don't really believe I can do this."

Get these potential obstacles down on paper, and then brainstorm strategies to keep them from stopping you. You might come up with approaches such as:

"I need to call a friend on Friday morning for a dose of support and encouragement before trying to fill out the application form that's due Monday."

"I need to avoid talking to my Mom until I complete the next task I've set, because her little cutting comments undermine my self-confidence whenever I try something new."

"I won't eat out for the next week so I can finally stop worrying about the cost of that doctor visit I've been avoiding."

"I'm going to put a sign on the mirror that says, 'Taking good care of myself is not selfishness. The world needs me to be well.'"

By focusing attention on likely obstacles, you can come up with ways to outsmart them.

Step 5: Gather Resource

This step involves three elements:

- Ask people for help.

- Find ways to draw more from inside yourself, increasing your inner resource.

- Find sources of assistance that you don't even have to ask for—they're just out there waiting for you.

Let's say that two years from now I want to bench press 180 pounds, which will require adhering strictly to twice-a-week workouts. My will power is strong, but it's not going to get me all the way to the finish line. So I start to gather the following resources:

Under "asking for help," I look for someone who would like to work out with me twice a week, asking around among my friends and putting up a notice at the gym.

Under "expanding my inner resource," I put up a chart at home and record my weights, sets, and reps after each workout, keeping it visible so I can draw inspiration from it daily.

Under "help that doesn't have to be asked for," I decide to pay for a few sessions (which is what I can afford) with a personal trainer to improve my lifting technique and training approach.

In this way, plan sources of support and energy that can keep you moving. You can follow through, despite what those voices in your head may say; but first you need the right plan in place.

Step 6: Feel And Release Your Feelings

Keep paying attention to what's happening inside you. Write in your journal, split time with a healing partner, take a thoughtful walk alone, open up with friends, and seize moments to laugh and cry.

Difficult feelings, including self-blame, will almost certainly come up at times when your progress is not what you had hoped. But they'll also come up due to progress you *are* making. The closer you get to achieving a long-awaited goal, the more you may encounter a tangle of emotions. Notice your feelings, get support for them, journal about them, and discharge them through your innate releases.

Step 7: The Check-In Process

Once you have goals in place, make a plan for regularly reflecting on your progress. If you have a goal-work partner, put dates on the calendar to check in with each other at least once a week. The check-in plan should include:

1) Review your goals. Are they still right for you? Do they need adjustments?

2) Celebrate what you've accomplished *even if it is less than you had hoped*. Always take stock of what you did do.

3) Examine pieces that you didn't reach (yet). Return to the question of external or internal obstacles that are holding

you back. Then recommit to carrying out those steps.

4) Consider gathering additional resource, especially for tasks that you're finding difficult.

5) Set goals to be done by the next check-in, continuing to include small, specific steps.

6) Don't dump on yourself about any of it. And modify your goals if they are turning out to be too big; this process is not about proving anything.

Key to the PLN approach to goal work is this:

When you don't meet a goal, including any intermediate tasks you had set, *there is to be no blame from your goal partner or from yourself.*

Criticism is not permitted anywhere in this process. The only acceptable response besides encouragement is *problem-solving*; if the plan didn't work, we need to *modify the plan*, not discredit the effort that was made. (And remember, "I'm going to try harder next time" is *not* a new plan. We've all tried that one countless times, and it almost never works.)

These are the only appropriate questions from the support person regarding unmet goals:

- *"What got in the way?"*

- *"How should we modify the plan so that it works better next time?"*

Take pride in your progress, however small. Mistaken thinking, promoted by sports coaches, bosses, and other overly demanding individuals, claims that if you feel proud or satisfied about your accomplishments, you won't work as hard in the future. This belief is backwards; the more you value and celebrate what you've done, the more you'll be able to do well.[1]

Setting and Holding Directions

Lastly we'll look at a different kind of goal work, where:

1) we focus on the short term

2) we set goals that are focused more on our internal world than on visible actions

We call these short-term efforts "directions," since they aim us against the current of discouragement and habit.

Directions are best explained with an example. Let's say your mind tends to freeze up in high-pressure moments; you find yourself in situations where you're just burning to say something, but the words either come out all wrong or not at all. (Sound familiar? Most of us grapple with this at one time or another.)

To work on this challenge, you might decide that for the next seven days you will take the following direction:

"I'm a very clear thinker with important things to say."

What I mean by "take this direction" is that you commit to making this outlook your primary mental focus for the week. Repeat it to yourself several times a day, like a mantra, and try to *feel your way into it*, reaching for an inner part of you that recognizes the truth of the direction.

---

[1] Some people are propelled to big accomplishments by dissatisfaction and criticism, but they rip themselves and others to emotional shreds in the process. This should in no way be viewed as a success.

Moreover, strive to *behave* as if you believe it, even though a big part of you doesn't yet. Periodically ask yourself, "What would I do differently right now if I saw myself as clear-thinking and insightful?"

Setting directions is even more helpful in collaboration with a healing partner. When you set a direction with your co-counselor's attention, you then head into your week picturing your partner rooting for you to hold onto it. During your counseling turn, repeatedly say the direction aloud. Experiment with various tones of voice as you say it, observing the different feelings that come up. Processing those feelings will help you hold the direction during the week. People tend in particular to laugh while voicing the new attitude that the direction captures, and this laughter can help you succeed in holding it.

Practice saying the phrase aloud forcefully with your healing partner. Then repeat it in your mind—or aloud—with that same conviction during the week ahead.

A direction doesn't involve a task. As long as you remind yourself of the direction frequently and put effort into adopting it, the week counts as a triumph.

Here are examples of directions I've used or seen other people use:

"I'm a force to be reckoned with!" – for someone who is trying to overcome timidity

"Here I come!" – for someone who wants to work on being less afraid to be visible

"Wheee!" – for someone who feels too constricted and is trying to learn to relax and have fun

"I know what I know!" – for someone who falls into self-doubt or confusion in disagreements

"I'm an important person!" – for someone who tends to un-dervalue himself or herself

"I can run through fire!" – for someone who has to take scary steps in the week ahead

When coming up with a direction for yourself or your co-counselor:

- Make it as positive as you can.

- Look for ways to make it fun or funny (as in the "run though fire" or "wheee!" examples above). Humor and playfulness help to outwit our fears and inner critics.

- Keep it short and sweet.

- Play around with different wording until you hit upon a version that speaks to you.

- Experiment with your tone of voice; a direction can be matter-of-fact, funny, angry, defiant, or loving. Find what feels right for the week ahead.

Don't worry about the "keep it positive" guideline if you come up with a direction that makes you laugh. A co-counselor of mine once decided to go through his week saying to himself, "I'm not the dumbest person in history." The phrase made him laugh like crazy, the best antidote for anxiety. Plus the direction outwitted his crit-ical internal voices better than defensively asserting "I'm smart!" ever had. (There are many ways to creatively fool a distress pattern.)

Why do we hold a direction for just a week? The an-swer is that attempting to adopt a new outlook through will-power doesn't work long term, but it *can* succeed for briefer periods. This effort helps us make short-term gains, which in turn propel our healing forward. Holding directions is a great tool to add to your toolbox, and can be surprisingly fun.

A Few Closing Thoughts

Goal work moves us toward living from choice. We gain clarity about who we are, and about what we want for ourselves and our world. Setting goals puts us in touch with our *values* and *beliefs*, so that we can align our lives with our deepest selves. Finally, it gives us a clearer sense of mission, enhancing the meaning in our lives.

If the process starts to feel burdensome, your goals may be coming more from a sense of what you "should" do and less from what you actually want. Make this process about *the unfolding of your life*, not about "success." Pursue instead the goal of experiencing what *you would most like to experience in this life*, and of getting to see *your world grow and move* in that direction.

Key Points to Remember:

- Healing moves along better when your eyes are fixed on where you want to go next.

- Share your deep goals and dreams with your loved ones, co-counselors, and others you trust.

- You'll develop unstoppable momentum if you return to this goal-work process a few times each year.

Chapter Fifteen

Breaking Free of Addiction

All of us struggle with certain behaviors that we do over and over again even though we don't really want to. Something drives us to keep repeating the mistake, perhaps as often as every day, but on a deeper level we know we're not serving ourselves well. We're putting our physical or emotional health at risk but we can't seem to break the pattern.

Who hasn't struggled with a loop of this kind?

Addictive behaviors are a prime example of making decisions *on automatic*; they are the antithesis of living from choice. We feel in the grip of forces that are moving our arms and legs (and mouths) for us as if we were puppets. We keep saying, "This time don't reach for that piece of cake!" but soon find ourselves eating it anyhow. Then we're riddled with self-blame.

And this self-blame is part of the trap, because the more negatively we feel toward ourselves the better hold the addictive pattern gets on us.

As I've said earlier, trying harder isn't going to solve much, and blaming ourselves accomplishes even less. We've already tried both of those plenty. We need a new plan.

The Nature of Addiction

Addictive behaviors are, in their essence, pain medications;

that's why actual pain medications are so addictive. Any behavior that you're addicted to has served at some point to numb out feelings that were too much for you to handle. The behavior still plays a pain-killing role today, though the feelings it's now chasing away may be different from the ones it initially protected you from.

Behaviors that cause numbness lead to two problems. First, over time numbness becomes unwelcome; it is fundamentally an unpleasant sensation, though it appears pleasant in comparison to the pain that it's masking. When misery first goes away, its disappearance *feels like* pleasure. But it isn't; pleasure is completely different from the removal of pain.

There's an old joke about this, where someone asks a man why he's hitting himself in the head with a hammer and he answers, "Because it feels so good when I stop."

Part of the problem is that it's impossible to numb just one thing; numbness spreads. That's why people complain that the years are going by too fast, or that life feels unsatisfying, or that they feel disconnected from people or events. These are all side-effects of the numbness we developed in the past to get through bad times.

The other problem is that numbness, ironically, leads to pain. If you have a body part that lacks sensation, you're going to keep harming it by accident because the pain isn't there to warn you. Similarly, when you are emotionally numb you make mistakes you don't realize you're making; and as a result you wake up in deeper pain down the road. For example, you end up hurting other people through insensitivity and then find yourself in a life where you've driven everyone away; or you do harm to yourself because you don't care ("Who gives a s***?"), and then years later you have huge regrets about what you did to your life.

The Addictive Loop

Addictive behavior, then, masks pain in the short term but actually causes more pain in the longer term. What is the result? *Increased addiction.*

Here's a typical example: A person starts drinking heavily while in college but, unlike most of her friends, she doesn't ease up after graduation; years later she's still drinking almost every day and is seriously buzzed a couple of times a week. A number of difficulties are resulting. She's had dating partners that she's been excited about but they don't stick around more than a few months because her drinking gets to them after a while. She's had a DUI. She's constantly broke because she spends so much money on drinks at clubs—since her social life revolves around drinking.

All these problems are making her frustrated, depressed, and lonely, which leads her to drink even *more*. The increased drinking starts to drive away friends, not just dating partners, and her workplace is getting frustrated about how often she calls in sick or shows up late. Which makes her want to drink even more.

And so forth.

Although many of us don't have a problem as serious and obvious as hers, we all struggle with lower-grade versions of it. We chase away pain or emptiness with:

- shopping, fantasizing about the next thing we want to buy, making home improvements, and other purchases.

- building our status and wealth, "getting ahead," "succeeding."

- video screens, social media, Web surfing.

- overeating, unhealthful eating.

- causing constant drama in our lives and being drawn to unhealthy people.

- alcohol, drugs, caffeine, nicotine, sweets.

- risk-taking or self-harming behavior.

- superficial sex, pornography.

- filling our heads up with thoughts, keeping a constant internal chatter going, mental loops.

- obsessions and compulsions.

Web surfing is the perfect modern illustration of how addiction feeds on itself; the more low energy, depressed, and lonesome you feel from hours of staring into your phone or your computer, the *harder* it becomes to turn it off.

Why Can Painful Things Be Addictive?

Here's a story I've heard various version of over the years:

"I keep falling in love with people who aren't available; either they're in a relationship or they're unavailable in an emotional sense. I know I'm doing it even right while I'm doing it; I'm just so attracted to people who are unattainable. And the thing is I know some really nice (men/women), but those aren't the ones I fall for."

Why would we be drawn to keep repeating choices that cause us so much pain? The answer is that we do it *to mask even deeper, scarier pain that's stored inside of us* from old wounds. We sometimes even hurt ourselves physically as a way to drive away unbearable emotional distress.

Pleasure Is Not Addictive!

It's actually quite difficult to get addicted to something that's genuinely good for you. It isn't pleasure that hooks people, it's numbness. What *is* addictive is the *promise* of pleasure and the *illusion* of pleasure; those have great power to chase other feelings away.

Gambling is an apt example of an addictive activity that works by promising pleasure that hardly ever comes; it makes you feel like pleasure is just *about* to come.

Getting drunk is a good example of the illusion of pleasure. People who are drunk insist that they're having a great time, but when they look back on the experience a day or two later, it hasn't left them with anything. Alcohol-induced fun is hollow; it leads to emptiness, not to satisfaction. But while you're in it everything *seems* great.

Compare this with, for example, talking to someone who got a deep massage the day before, or who climbed a mountain to a beautiful view. Ask them what was left in the wake of their experience, and they'll say it's left a lasting glow for a day or two, that they can feel it doing good things inside of them. Genuine pleasure is good for us, and the effects last.

Even with addictions to things that are truly pleasurable, like food or sex, it's still not the pleasure that the person is addicted to. People aren't addicted to eating, they're addicted to overeating, which actually feels bad. People aren't addicted to sex, they're addicted to superficial sex that lacks real human connection, which is an empty experience.

When people try to break free of a serious addiction, they feel like they're giving up their dearest friend and greatest source of pleasure; but once it's all behind them, they feel that nothing much was actually lost. That's the irony: the thing we're having such a hard time giving up is something we neither want nor need, and it's actually making us feel bad, not good.

Modern society across much of the world has become negative about pleasure. It gets portrayed as sinful, superficial, or addictive. *Pleasure is not the problem*; in fact, on the deepest level pleasure is what life is all about. The reality is that the more sources we have of truly satisfying sensory and emotional experiences, the less we're drawn to addictive behaviors.

Examining the Things You Think You Like

The first step to breaking free of addictive behaviors, then, is this:

Start paying closer attention to your own feelings, both during and after life experiences. Begin to notice which things bring you genuine, lasting pleasure. Notice at the same time if there are things that you've always thought of as pleasurable that actually turn out not to be once you examine your feelings and reactions more carefully.

Here's an example of where this reflecting can lead: Many years ago I started tuning into my feelings while I was eating sweets, which I had always thought I loved. I soon realized that what I felt was actually mostly an unpleasant hyperness (many addictive behaviors bring anxiety and hyperness). I also felt an overwhelming desire to keep eating more sweets; it was impossible to have enough until I'd had too much. In short, I was feeling desperation but hardly any actual pleasure. I proceeded to stop eating sweets for good, not for health reasons but because I realized they made me feel bad.

The second key point is this:

Breaking free of an addiction does not involve giving up anything important; the sense of loss is an illusion. We're actually delighted when the addiction is gone.

The third key point is:

When we feel a high level of emotional pain, or a high level of emotional emptiness (which is a kind of pain), the experience of numbness will be such a huge relief that we'll come to think of numbness as pleasure and start to confuse the two.

And last:

*Addictive behavior ultimately causes an **increase** of the pain and emptiness that we're trying to escape, causing a vicious circle.*

So let's learn the way out of here.

Recognizing Addiction

Here are some clues to patterns that we're hooked on:

- We often feel regretful after we engage in the behavior.
- We feel embarrassed or secretive about things we have done.
- We're having negative financial or work performance effects from it.
- We've had friends or partners distance themselves from us because of it.
- We're focused on wanting to be really sure we can fit the behavior into our day somewhere.

- We make excuses for engaging in the addictive behavior, blaming people in our lives, our financial stresses, or how hard our lives are.

- We're choosing our friends and intimate partners on the basis of who shares the behavior or won't raise concerns with us about it.

- A voice inside us tells us that it isn't good for us, and we're having internal battles with ourselves about that.

Addictive behaviors are not the same as *healthful coping mechanisms*. You may find, for example, that it's really crucial to your mental health to get solid exercise every day. If you wake up in the morning and start thinking right away about how you're going to fit in a workout, that's not a sign of an addiction; that's a sign of taking good care of yourself

Don't start questioning yourself about everything you enjoy doing; we need more pleasure in our lives, not less. As long as you don't ignore signals that a certain behavior isn't good for you, you're fine.

The Underrecognized Role of Emptiness

Emptiness is a particular kind of pain that gnaws away inside of us even if we're barely aware of it. It plays a much bigger role in addiction than most people realize. While some people develop addictions to block overt pain, many others are battling hidden distresses: meaninglessness, dissatisfaction, hunger for love, hunger for physical affection, hunger for community. In short, they are *longing*. These are the rampant distresses of the modernized world. If you're battling addictive behaviors, check in with yourself to see if any of these hidden corrosives are taking their toll on you, and apply the approaches from this book to addressing them.

How Addictive Behaviors Interfere with Healing

Addictive behaviors take important pieces of our feelings away. Over time we start to be generally numb or to get locked into oscillating between pain and numbness, with those poles becoming what life is all about.

Healing and growth require an ability to tolerate uncomfortable feelings. People who don't feel don't grow. You may know someone who has been drinking or drugging since they were only 12 or 14 years old, and twenty or thirty years later they still have the maturity and responsibility of a 12-year-old. The substance has drawn the person's development to a halt.

People who abuses substances occasionally have what seem to be *huge* breakthroughs psychologically. They appear to suddenly look at their lives honestly and clearly, to gain tremendous insight, and to gather the inner strength to make big changes. These epiphanies can cause the person's loved ones to get their hopes up that the person is finally going to escape the addiction. But a year later the person has the same breakthrough. And four months after that they have it again. And two years later another one. The loop just goes on and on and nothing actually breaks through.

Interference With Emotional Release

For some reason when people release pain under the influence of a substance *nothing gets permanently discharged.*

Alcoholics are famous for crying and crying, and it goes nowhere. The healing effects of the other forms of discharge are blocked as well; for example, laughing fits on drugs or alcohol demonstrably do not lead to any lasting relief or change.

The more general way in which addictive behaviors interfere is that they keep us from releasing pain in the first place. When a big cry is coming on and we reach for the ice cream, or the wine, or superficial sex, then the cry is not going to come. We never feel what we need to feel and never release what we need to release.

Overcoming Addiction

Now the road map: We can combine the concepts we've just covered about addiction with healing principles from the prior chapters, and find our way out of these loops.

1. Increase your internal awareness.

Pay more attention to how you feel, including observing which life activities help you to feel deep feelings versus the ones that chase feelings away. Start also tuning into the dynamics of emptiness and longing, which are more subtle than other kinds of pain but no less powerful.

2. Find people you trust with whom you can break silence regarding the behavior.

Opening up is essential. You've got to stop keeping it secret to have any chance of getting out of it.

3. Find structured one-on-one support.

"Structured support" is support that occurs on a schedule and has a set format. My first recommendation, of course, is that you co-counsel with someone regularly. Devote a substantial portion of your session time to issues surrounding the behavior pattern you're wanting to escape. Strive to describe the entire process without holding anything back, including:

- the kinds of feelings you have as your desire to engage in the behavior builds.

- your fantasies about the behavior, such as planning for your next time doing it.

- the feelings that come up for you when you try *not* to do it.

- what you're experiencing, both good and bad, while involved in the behavior.

- what your fears are of life without the behavior.

- what you feel ashamed of regarding the behavior.

Leave as little unexpressed as possible; *addiction thrives on secrecy and shame.*

Notice that your healing partner still cares about you and believes in you. Your internal voices are telling you that anyone who knew the truth would take a negative view of you, and it's not true. Take in the fact that you're still loved despite what you've revealed.

At the same time, your support person shouldn't be telling you, "It's not so bad, it's no big deal, everybody does stuff like that." Collusion is not support. The best support comes in the form of, "*I really love and care about you, and it's*

clear that your addictive behavior is not okay and has to change."
You need people who care about you to approach you with:

1) Unconditional love

2) A recognition that overcoming an addiction is a difficult process that comes with a lot of work and setbacks, and that on some level you've been doing the best you can so far

3) An insistence that you can, and must, do better

You need someone who can give you support for your *emotions*, including how incredibly hard this all is, but at the same time *not* give you support for your excuses.

If you're in the helping role, bear in mind you have zero control over whether the addicted person is going to break free or not. All you can do is offer the three elements I just listed; the rest is out of your hands.

If you're the one battling the destructive habit, you don't get to put any of the blame on people who—in your opinion—are not supporting you in the right way. You won't break out of your pattern as long as you make it anyone else's responsibility.

I recommend that you contract with your healing partner that you'll focus largely on the addiction issues during your sessions for several months or more. (And if you haven't found a healing partner yet, go on the PLN website and start the process.) If you decide to work with a professional therapist, seek one out that specializes in addiction recovery.

4. Find structured group support

Depending on the particular pattern you're battling group support may be easy or difficult to find. If your issue is with substance abuse, gambling, or overeating, the 12-Step programs (such as Alcoholics Anonymous) are widely available. There may also be Rational Recovery groups near you, which have a different approach from the 12-Step programs and are a better fit for some people.

You can also find addiction groups through local hospitals, mental health centers, and substance abuse clinics which follow a range of philosophies. There are also PLN groups forming both regionally and online that are addiction-specific; go to the forum at PeakLivingNetwork.org to learn more. If you can't find anything there for your issue, put up a post to get something started.

Some people use addiction groups like AA to hang around with other addicts and stay stuck, so be sure to scope out which people are serious about doing the work and surround yourself quickly with those folks. Visit meetings at different times and locations to see where you think people are making real progress.

5. Include the following specific pieces of healing work in your process.

In your one-one-one sessions, group meetings, and journal writing, look for opportunities to explore the following issues:

- *Shame.* See what memories come up of times when you were shamed by adults or older children when you were growing up. Just as important, look at present-time feelings of shame that you struggle with, especially ones that you feel after you engage in addictive behavior. Feeling ashamed of your patterns is a key element of the glue that keeps you stuck in them.

You need to do the somewhat tricky work of becoming more self-forgiving on the one hand, while not allowing yourself to rationalize and minimize your behavior on the other.

- *The impact that other people's addictions have had on us.* Leftover wounds from growing up around addicted adults can be a driving force in the next generation's addictions. Explore the question of what your parents and other relatives were addicted to and how their addictions harmed you, how addiction affected your friends (beginning during your teen years), and who in your current life is driven by addiction. Pay attention to processing and releasing your grief and anger from these experiences, which are feeding your own addiction.

- *How our addictions have affected other people.* Facing and dealing with the harm we've done to others makes us less ashamed, not more so, and thus is part of the escape route. Besides, it's our responsibility.

- *Everything you can remember about your life and feelings around the time you first started behaving in the addicted way.* There are big emotional clues back at the beginning. Spend time digging around in your memories of the period in your life when you started down the road into this trap.

- *Grieve the loss of the addiction as you would a friend who died.* Use the following technique in a series of co-counseling sessions: Form an image of your addiction as a companion you've loved but that you are now going to part from. Explain aloud, as if that companion were in the room, why you have to leave ("because my health is declining, because you're causing me to make big mistakes" and so forth). Express how sorry you are to go, but that at this point in your life it's an absolutely necessary choice. Say "good-bye" over and over again, aloud. See what feelings this brings up and work with those extensively. And if tears, laughter, or rage start to come, let them grow and flow as much as they can; release remains the top priority when working on addiction, just as with any other issue.

6. Pay attention to what you need to add, not just what you need to take away.

We think of escaping addiction as being about icily denying ourselves something we intensely crave. But what if it's equally about warmly giving *to* ourselves? What if much of the work is about getting clearer about what we truly love and desire, and getting *more* of that into our lives? What if it's about being loving with ourselves rather than about being hard on ourselves?

An addiction is a hyperactive salesperson dedicated to selling us a product that does nothing for us. "YOU NEED THIS!" it screams for hours at a time, "YOU'D BE MISERABLE WITHOUT THIS! YOU NEED EVEN MORE! NEXT TIME IT WILL FINALLY BE ENOUGH, SO DON'T STOP!!"

Amidst all this noise it's hard to think about what we actually want and to find where our hearts truly lie. Chapter 17, "Refilling the Human Well," will guide you to answer the crucial question, *"What is it that I really need?"*

Begin reflecting on this theme, exploring it with your support system and in your journal. Make it part of your daily routine to ask yourself, "What are the things that most matter to me, and how can I work more pieces of them into my day?" Explore what makes you happy, but also what fulfills you on a deeper level and gives you a sense of purpose.

7. Get away from people who are toxic to you or draw you into staying stuck.

Any addiction recovery program will tell you the importance of examining your social circle, which may need an overhaul. Take a look at whether:

- you're hanging out largely with people who share your addiction or a related one.

- you're spending a lot of time with people who demand nothing from you so that you're not challenged in any way, while avoiding people who try to get you to deal with your addiction.

- you're doing the opposite of the last one, being around people who criticize you, throw the past up in your face, give little digs that make you feel bad about yourself, and generally keep you down.

- you're often around people out of a sense of obligation (unhealthy relatives, for example, or friends with whom you have a long history) when you know they aren't good for you; you know you need to move on but you feel as though you'd be betraying your people.

- you sense that people around you actually don't really want you to get well; they seem to feel threatened if you start to make progress and they lure you back toward unhealthful behavior.

- you have an abusive or controlling partner or parent, and you're staying addicted as a way to manage the pain of what that person is doing to you.

If you don't distance yourself from the toxic people in your life, your chances of making lasting changes are small. You don't have to feel like you're abandoning people. Think of it more as taking a break—perhaps as much as a year or two—until you can get yourself solidly on the road to freedom from addiction. Then you can carefully add these people back into your life if you choose to, but give them a smaller role than before and don't let them threaten your balance.

Remember, don't compromise your growth out of feeling guilty toward the people you've left behind; *they always have the option to get well if they choose to*. And if they do, you'll make a place for them in your life.

Two Closing Thoughts

The distinction between addictions and other unwanted patterns is not always clear and isn't necessarily important. If you have a recurring behavior that's interfering with your health, your enjoyment of life, or your relationships, it's time for it to go. Don't get hung up on what fits the definition of an addiction and what doesn't; the principles that I've covered in this chapter will work for you either way.

Freedom from addiction is like freedom from a cage. Talk to anyone who has escaped, and they will tell you:

- how much more they now enjoy life.

- how much lighter and freer they feel.

- how wonderful it is not to walk around carrying shame and secrecy.

- how life then and life now are like night and day.

- how, although they sometimes miss certain entertaining aspects of the addicted life, they wouldn't trade their new life for the old one *for anything.*

Remember that it *seems* like you're losing something, but no real loss is involved. When you come out the other end of the battle, you'll find that you have only gained, and gained a lot.

Key Points to Remember:

- All of us have had addictive patterns at some point.

- Truly satisfying, pleasurable activities are rarely addictive. Pleasure is not our enemy.

- An addiction can be harder to overcome than other behavior patterns, but if we make a plan that takes that challenge into account, we can succeed.

Chapter Sixteen

Escaping and Healing From Abuse

Almost all of us have lived at some point in our lives with daily or near-daily exposure to someone who systematically tears us down. The person has verbally abused us, been mentally cruel, hurt us physically or threatened to do so, cut us off from other people, controlled us like a dictator. And then to top it all off the person has blamed us for all of these behaviors, ultimately bullying us into blaming ourselves.

The abusive person could be:

- your parent

- your intimate partner or former partner

- your employer or supervisor

- your adult child (when you're a middle-aged or elderly parent)

- a superior in a hierarchical organization such as the military

- a judge, child protective worker, police officer, or other person who has societal power over you

Abuse is so rampant that it's important for anyone participating in the Peak Living Network to develop sensitivity to what people with abuse histories are dealing with.

Key Concept #1: Entrapment

An abusive person has access to power over you so that you can't easily escape the abuse. If you could, you would. If you're being abused by a boss, for example, you struggle with several questions that impinge on your freedom:

"Can I find another job quickly? If not, how will I survive? Will this boss sabotage my efforts to get other jobs?"

"How can I make sure to provide for my children?"

"How will it look on my work history if I leave this job? How will that affect my future?"

"What impact will it have on my clients if I quit? How will it affect my co-workers?"

"What happens to my/our health insurance? My retirement? My car payments? My rent?"

"Is the way I'm being treated my own fault? If so, what good will it do try to go somewhere else?"

An abusive boss understands that you face these traps; that's how he or she gets away with mistreating you and other people at the workplace.

The entrapment element is always present. Abused children are completely trapped because they have no legal say over where they live or with whom. If child welfare becomes involved, those personnel decide whether the child leaves the home, where and for how long he or she is placed, and when the child is returned; the child still has no say at all. Most children would rather stay at home with abusive parents than be cast into other circumstances of complete powerlessness where, among other losses, they are typically separated from their siblings.

The elderly are often trapped by physical limitations, health problems, limited income, and isolation. Intimate partners are trapped by threats, by isolation, by lack of access to money, by trauma, and by lack of societal support for leaving. When a woman has children with a man who is abusing her, leaving him means that she will have to sacrifice much of her relationship with her children because family courts usually require abused mothers to share custody.

My central message to the abused person: Reflect on the factors that are trapping you. Don't blame yourself for being trapped. You can find a way out, but it will take some time. The better you understand what's holding you there, the better your chance to figure out the path to freedom.

My central message to the support person: People do not get stuck in abuse because of being masochistic. They get stuck because the abuser (along with the society that backs that abuser up) has trapped them in myriad ways. Offering simple solutions won't help because there are no simple solutions. You become much more helpful when you grasp how complex it all is.

Key Concept #2: Abusers Tell You It's Your Own Fault

An abuser doesn't necessarily blame you for every single incident—they may even act apologetic sometimes—but their overall behavior pattern always includes repeated efforts to make you feel that you're the cause of the abuse. The result is that virtually every person who has lived with abuse comes to feel that they are at fault, partially or entirely, for what's been done to them. They feel that they pushed the abuser's buttons, or that their mistakes and misbehavior caused the abuser to turn mean. They feel they should have stood up to the person more—or should have done so less. *All of these messages are the voice of the abuser speaking through the mind of the person being abused.*

In reality, nothing an abused person can do will make the abuser treat them any better. Abusive behavior comes *entirely* from factors that are *internal* to the abusive person, and not at all from anything about the personality, behavior, or responses of the targeted person, whether adult or child.

Effects of abuse are often mistaken for causes of abuse. For example, children who live with abuse often develop hostile, defiant, and even violent behavior patterns. The abusive adult then blames his or her mistreatment of the child on the child's bad behavior. This reversal of cause and effect is equally rampant in intimate partner abuse, elder abuse, and abuse by employers.

My central message to the abused person: You are doing nothing—zero—to cause the way you're being treated. If there are serious problems in your own behavior, you should work to improve those for your own sake and for the sake of other people in your life; but doing so will not do anything about *the abuser's* conduct. The abuser is 100% responsible for his or her own behavior, and you can't make it change.

My central message to the support person: Blaming an abused person for the abuser's behavior, or for the circumstances brought about by that behavior, never helps. The way out comes from supporting and empowering the target of the abuse, not by blaming or criticizing him or her.

Be alert to the way that abusive people manipulate the question of responsibility. When an abusive partner is called out on his actions, for example, he says resentfully, "Oh, so you're saying I'm the cause of all the tensions in our relationship, that everything that's gone wrong between us is my fault." He's skillfully changing the subject so that instead of being about his abusive actions it's about "the tensions in our relationship" and "the things that have gone wrong between us." The proper response from the rest of us is, "We're not talking about 'the relationship' or 'the tensions.' We're talking about *your behavior*. And, yes, you are 100% responsible for your own actions."

Key Concept #3: Yes, It Is That Bad

I very often hear targets of abuse saying, "I'm probably making too big a deal about this," or, "I'm sure I'm blowing this all out of proportion." This is, again, the voice of the abuser speaking through the abused person; abusive people are fond of telling their targets that they're unstable, that they overreact, that they make something out of nothing. Don't buy it.

My central message to the abused person: Take your feelings seriously. When someone tells you that you're overreacting to how they're treating you, it's important to be highly suspicious of that claim. Trust your own instincts.

My central message to the support person: Keep validating the person's feelings. Keep pointing out his or her strengths and accomplishments. Support targets of abuse to believe in themselves.

Key Concept #4: Isolation Is an Enemy, Connection Is a Friend

Abuse thrives where people feel alone, and abusers work hard to keep their targets isolated.

This is a realm in which our survival strategies, which are so crucial to our well-being, can unfortunately get in our way. One way we get through painful or scary situations is to keep telling ourselves, "I can handle this, I can handle this." At a certain point this helpful message stops being positive and switches over to harming us—because the reality of our circumstances is that we desperately need help. And it's okay to need help—in fact it's profoundly human to give and receive assistance, to need one another.

So when you're dealing with an abusive person in your life there's a point where it becomes a positive message to tell yourself, "I can't deal with this—this is too much for me." It's time to reach out for help, as scary or humiliating as that may feel.

The abused person sometimes says, "I can't really go for help because my own behavior is part of the problem." This is backwards thinking; *if you are feeling disturbed by your own behavior, that in itself is a sure sign that you can't handle the situation on your own*. Accept the fact that you need assistance.

Find someone to whom you can tell the truth about what's happening. Take the leap to trust someone. Check books and check on the Web for information about the particular kind of mistreatment that you're facing. Build your social connection in whatever way you can. Breaking out of isolation takes courage and creativity, but it's the single most important step you can take to change your future.

My central message to the abused person: You don't have to be alone and it isn't good for you. Don't listen to the abuser when he/she blames you for why you feel so alone. Keep finding ways to reach out to people and never give up.

My central message to the support person: Connect, connect, connect. Be there, be there, be there. Helping the abused person overcome isolation is the most valuable contribution you can make. Work to govern your own frustration and impatience because those will keep you from being fully connected to the person you're trying to support.

Key Concept #5: You Will Find Your Way Out

If you seek out support and information, you'll eventually find your way to freedom. The abusive person tries to convince you that you're crazy, incompetent, selfish, and helpless, and that no one cares about you or likes you. And under the impact of all that abuse, some of these accusations may start to seem true about you, but they're not. There is nothing wrong with you. You'll find a way to an abuse-free life and to heal from the harm that's been done. It can feel like you'll be there forever, but you won't be.

My central message to the abused person: You are smart, capable, and sane. You will get free and be surrounded once again by people who love you, believe in you, and are kind to you.

My central message to the support person: Keep reflecting back to the abused person all of the positive qualities you see in him or her. Keep believing that s/he will get free.

What If the Abusive Person Says That You're The Abusive One?

Abusers specialize in turning the tables on their targets. You can feel like the word is turning upside down when the abusive person tells you that *you're* the one who's controlling, who doesn't show respect, who's selfish, and so forth. *You will never win this argument.* It doesn't matter how perfectly you make your points to prove that you're not the one being abusive, the abusive person will *always* have something to come back with.

The only solution is to let go of trying to make the person see. Focus instead on how to lessen the person's impact on your life and mind.

Next Steps

The Peak Living Network is committed to being an environment where survivors of all types of abuse are supported, believed, and understood. Please take some time to inform yourself on these issues even if you're one of the fortunate people who has not been a target. Here are some beginning places for finding more information:

Abusive Relationship Partners

I recommend that you start at **LundyBancroft.com**. My professional website offers a very extensive listing of books, videos, and websites under the "Resources" tab.

My own books include *Why Does He Do That?: Inside the Minds of Angry and Controlling Men*, which has become the go-to book for women in relationships with abusive or controlling partners, and *Daily Wisdom for 'Why Does He Do That': Encouragement for Women Involved with Angry and Controlling Men* which is a book of 365 short daily inspirational readings for abused women.

Another great beginning resource is the book *The Verbally Abusive Relationship* by Patricia Evans.

Abusive Parents

I recommend starting with *Toxic Parents* by Susan Forward. I also really like the HAVOCA website, **Havoca.org**. And for survivors of child sexual abuse (whether the perpetrator was a parent or not), there is Angela Shelton's awesome site **SurvivorManual.com**.

Abusive Adult Children (Targeting Their Aging Parents)

I like the information at the Help Guide website, **helpguide.org/articles/abuse/elder-abuse-and-neglect.htm**.

A book that gets excellent reviews is *The Family Guide to Preventing Elder Abuse* by Thomas Lee Wright.

Unfortunately, most resources on elder abuse are written for social workers, not directly for the elderly person or for his or her loved ones. For example, someone recently drew to my attention how hard it is to find information and support if you're concerned that one of your siblings is abusing your aging parent.

Abuse by Employers

The best of the books out there on this subject seems to be *Prisoners of a Hostile Work Environment* by Curt Kosterman, which focuses on calling workplace abuse what it is and exploring strategies for fighting back.

The best online information I've found is at the Workplace Bullying Institute, **WorkplaceBullying.org**.

I'm concerned by how many of the resources out there (not including the ones I just listed) focus on strategies for getting along with your abusive boss—which will never work for long—instead of providing validation for the worker and analysis of the dynamics. We're living under an economic system where workers have almost no rights but writers are avoiding saying that, and we can't solve a problem that we're not naming.

Abuse by Superior Officers

The best information I've found so far is at **GIrightshotline.org**.

Members of the military have extremely limited rights, which is a serious problem in itself. When I have done research on abuse by superior officers, a lot of what I find says, "Well, if the officer is giving you a legal order, there's nothing you can do about it." But go to the website and learn as much as you can.

If You Chronically Mistreat Other People

If you have a pattern of abusive or mean behavior yourself, changing that behavior needs to be your highest priority. The first step is to stop denying it and stop blaming other people for it; the excuses you make will keep you stuck in the pattern endlessly. You can take charge of putting yourself on a different path. Read the article "How to Stop

Harming Others" at PeakLivingNetwork.org, and get to work on the steps there.

A Final Note: Abusers Who Masquerade As Victims

Abusive people can be drawn to presenting themselves as victims of abuse; they enjoy the attention, and the support for their denial, that they get when everyone who hears their story feels bad for them. Our default outlook in the Peak Living Network is to believe people's reports of having been abused. However, there are a couple of situations where we need to be cautious with our support in case we're being given the story in a distorted and perhaps reversed way:

1) *Cases where the power dynamics are reversed*. These involve, for example, an adult man saying that he's being abused by a woman, or a boss saying he or she is being abused by an employee. Reports of this kind can be real but they're very often not. For example, some abusive men can be way into talking about their feelings and their "vulnerability," so that everyone thinks, "Oh, he couldn't be an abuser, he's too sensitive."

2) *Cases where your gut keeps telling you that something is wrong with the story*. When this happens don't start treating the person as if they're not telling the truth, but don't ignore what your gut is telling you either.

In either of the above cases, proceed with caution, learn more about the situation, and see what unfolds. The story may turn out to be bona fide, but our inner signals are sometimes picking up on something important. In the Peak

Living Network we want to be loving and supportive, but we also want to be smart and on the side of the oppressed. Let's avoid letting abusive people manipulate us.

Key Points to Remember:

- Abuse has certain core characteristics that are always present in one form or another.

- Abuse is about someone using their power over you to hurt and control you.

- When the abusive person tell you that you're causing them to behave the way they do, that is 100% false.

- Getting free can take time, but you'll find a way.

- To be able to heal well from abuse, you'll need to get away from it.

Chapter Seventeen

Refilling the Human Well

A vibrant, challenging life is the context in which healing flourishes. Taking action to improve our lives on the one hand, and giving attention to our emotional healing on the other, are two rock climbers alternating on the lead as they scale a mountain; a burst of progress from one creates the context for a surge upward from the other, the two taking turns opening up the route. Risk and rest, joy and sadness, independence and protection, bounce back and forth against one another as we rise toward fulfillment.

To be fully emotional healthy, then, we have to learn not only how to heal from injury but how to stay well in the first place. What are our true needs, the essential elements that we all need to build into our lives to keep ourselves emotionally healthy? And how do we learn to identify things we think we need but that actually we'd be better off without?

Love

Beyond basic physical necessities for food, water, shelter, and sleep, there is nothing human beings crave more than love. Children who are loved without reservation are happier and more secure. They have an easier time with transitions, whether personal ones like potty-training or family ones such as moving to a new home. The relationships they form, as children and in their adult lives, are closer and more numerous. Adults who feel loved, especially unconditionally so, cope better with stress and grief and feel higher levels of overall life satisfaction.

Love galvanizes our physical health as well; in the words of Dr. Bernie Siegel, "unconditional love is the most powerful known stimulant of the immune system."

So is it unhealthful to be single? No. Romantic love sometimes works wonders, at least for periods of time, but it is neither necessary nor sufficient for well-being. People who are single are not necessarily lonely, and those who are in couples sometimes feel very isolated. What counts is the presence in our lives of multiple people who are supportive, who listen well, and who share their emotional selves with us.

Unconditional love does not mean generic love. We want to feel that the people in our lives care about us because of the *specific* people we are. It feels so good when someone notices our intelligence, or our creativity, or our courage, or our generosity. (Praise for our appearance or our possessions doesn't touch us as deeply since it isn't about who we are.)

Unconditional love also does not mean love that sets no limits. We should insist on being well-treated by friends and lovers, and they should insist on the same from us. We may even be forced at times to cut off contact with a loved one because of how toxic they are to us, though we can continue to love them from afar.

Love that is not expressed is love lost. It's regrettably possible to move through our days never realizing how much we have meant to certain people and never saying what they have meant to us. We all need to hear it.

Giving Love

We long to give love as much as to receive it, and to feel that our love for others *matters*. Children as young as two years old show this drive in the elaborate care they give to baby dolls and stuffed animals and in their desire to express love to the people who are important to them. Young children don't want to be *responsible* for other people—they're not ready for that—but they do want to shower their love and *have that love treasured*. So while they shouldn't hear from an adult, "I don't know where I'd be without you," they thrill at the words, "Your love is so precious to me."

Loving feelings that we've been unable to share leave a residue of anguish as great as any unmet need. The classic Steinbeck novel *East of Eden* is the story of a teenage boy's increasing pain and desperation as his father repeatedly rebuffs the love and assistance that the boy tenders. He wants more than anything to have his father accept and value his contributions.

The desire to give love and to nurture becomes even greater with age. We want to see that our love can inspire, that it can energize, that it can heal. There is no music more delightful than hearing someone say to us, "My life has really changed for the better since you came into it." If you're frustrated that people in your life are not accepting the transformative power of your love, that doesn't mean that you're "co-dependent;" more likely you're just in need of people who are willing and able to receive.

We feel an inherent desire to watch the growth of the next generation and to be involved in the care and guidance of the young. When we go through periods in our life where we have no regular contact with children, it's entirely natural that we feel that something important is missing.

Caring and being cared for need to be in balance. Constant giving drains us, while passive receiving leaves us feeling like victims in need of rescue.

The healing power of *giving* love is missing for the client in professional therapy; a therapist is not supposed to let you make a difference in his or her life. One of the reasons for the healing power of co-counseling relationships is that their structure brings *loving* and *being loved* into their proper equilibrium.

You have so much to give. Hold nothing back.

Physical Affection

Touch is as basic a human need as food and water. Studies (performed by twisted individuals) have demonstrated what happens to monkeys—close relatives of ours—when they are isolated from physical contact: they become emotional wrecks, physically unhealthy, and violent.

Touch is one of the driving forces in healing. Put a hand on someone who is crying and he or she cries harder. Let a trembling person lean against you and the shakes get more pronounced. Being able to hold onto someone tightly helps us through life's most painful events.

Human beings need far more contact than we get in modern society. We need frequent hugs, an arm around the shoulder, a hand wrapped in ours. And at least once in a while we need the chance to hold tightly to someone for a long time, to be cuddled up.

Touch is only nurturing, though, when the person being touched wants the contact and when the person doing the touching is thoughtful and respectful. Each of us has the right to determine who can touch us and how we are to be touched. No child should ever be told, "You need to give me a hug goodnight," or, "Give grandma a kiss." No child should be touched sexually, and no one of any age should be pressured into sexual contact or other unwanted intimacy.

Your body belongs to you, and you have the right to decide for yourself, free from any outside pressure, how physically close to get to anyone. When our bodies are in our control—and only then—they are tremendous vehicles for communicating love and facilitating healing.

Sexuality

We live in a period when sexuality has been heavily repressed. In our times most people have grown up with learned shame about their bodies and about the pursuit of physical pleasure. There's nothing wrong with your body, and nothing sinful about your enjoyment of your body's sensations. The only wrongs in sexuality come if you are hurting or taking advantage of someone else (which includes any sexual contact between adult and child). Bodies and physical pleasure are inherently wonderful, both in sexual and non-sexual forms.

Sexuality doesn't seem in itself to be an essential emotional need, but it's a wonderful avenue for fulfilling the basic needs for affection, pleasure, and intimacy. People who don't have sex in their lives can be completely emotionally well by finding other sources of warm affection and cuddling, and other ways to get pleasure from their bodies.

Managing Mixed Feelings About Touch

Past abuses and violations can make us feel unsafe with close physical contact and can make the sensation of being touched unpleasant. But if we can't participate in physical affection we face a significant obstacle since healing is so touch-dependent. Here are some guidelines for navigating that tension:

- Listen carefully to internal messages that tell you not to have physical contact with certain people, and honor those. Don't feel obligated to have an explanation, for yourself or for the other person, about why you want to keep your space.

- At the same time, if your internal messages are telling you not to touch *anyone*, you'll want to look for ways to safely push through that *over time*.

- Sometimes, especially (but not only) for survivors of sexual abuse, a period of literally not touching anyone actually is best. You'll be able to sense when it's the right time to start gently exploring a move back toward touch; don't rush it.

Attention

Try sitting next to an infant for a few minutes while keeping your face and eyes averted. After a while you'll sense the infant's mounting discomfort; she or he wants to see your face, wants to feel the attention of your eyes. Nothing else will do. Babies are more interested in the configuration of the human face than in any other pattern.

Adults need attention too. We can't function in top form, emotionally or intellectually, unless we're listened to well, our opinions respected and our emotions validated. Like infants, we need to be looked at; eye contact is more important than any other factor in determining whether a person who is speaking feels listened to. We feel better when we get a chance to share what our days have been like, to discuss our goals and dreams, to open up about our feelings, to show the fruits of our work.

Self-Expression

Expressing our feelings and thoughts, and telling the stories of what has happened to us, are among our fundamental needs. We need to tell the truth about our experiences and share our inner worlds with other people in ways that help us sense that others really "get it." We need to recount our pains and joys. We need someone to know.

Spoken words are only one way to capture reality. Look for ways to get your stories across through drawings, poems and songs, pottery, a piece of theater.

Telling is linked to remembering; we can only share as much as we know about what we have lived. But sharing also unlocks our recall; the more we tell the more we remember.

Play

Play is not just kids' stuff. Adult mammals of all kinds not only play with their young but can also be observed at play by themselves or with other adults. Polar bears of all ages, for example, love to climb snowy hillsides and slide down them.

Play can be all-consuming, with everything ceasing to exist but the game. Pleasure and imagination permeate the atmosphere, and our senses are vibrantly alive. Our earliest moments of theatrical play are the beginning of mysticism, of invented worlds that feel so real that we can physically move inside of them. Play broadens our engagement with the world; I may be a child growing up in Iowa, but at the same time I can be an explorer in a cave, a Russian ballet dancer, a parent of many children. And why should adults have any less need than children to crawl through tunnels on hands and knees, to act silly and laugh, to explore their senses?

Play has been corrupted by competition, to the point where some children and most adults have become incapable of playing a game that isn't competitive. Competition doesn't need to be eliminated but it has to stop being the only way we know how to play.

Adults tend to avoid playing because they don't want to be seen "acting like a child," a fear that's born of society's profound devaluing of children. We all need to overcome our inhibitions and rejoin the mystical world of imagination, freedom, and pleasure to which play is the doorway. Our children can teach us how.

Independence

Each of us needs a sense of personal competence and ability to navigate the world, whether adult or child, male or female. The craving for independence is universal.

Independence is mistakenly thought of as meaning "not needing anything from anyone else," as if the strongest person were the one who learns to do without. Deprivation is not empowering. Self-confidence comes from *taking charge of getting our needs met*, not from learning not to need anything. Define your independence in terms of *what you can do* not in terms of *what you can do without*. Define your own goals, not allowing anyone else to run your life, but then gather allies to propel you towards them.

Human closeness and personal power are not in contradiction; each one works to make the other possible. Our long-term goal, in other words, is *interdependence*.

Solitude

Solitude is a centering experience. Quiet reflection sorts our own thoughts out from other people's. Free from the pressure to please, impress, or persuade, our minds can wander down their own chosen paths.

Take breaks from the barrage of stimulus that the world aims at you. Turn off your phone (yes, it will be okay), put down the magazine, turn off the television; just think, or daydream, or doodle. Take a walk to clear your head, ideally in a pretty place. Ride your bike, go for a drive, retreat to the cellar to work on your dollhouse. Write in a journal, an ancient form of solitary refection that brings rest, strength, and clarity.

Solitary reflection will sometimes lead you to the solutions to problems. Our minds function best when we get time to think together with other people and then also get time to quietly follow our own thoughts.

Time spent alone brings you into a more intimate relationship with yourself. It helps you redraw your boundaries, so that you keep track of where you end and others begin. Value your relationship with yourself.

Creativity

There is no such thing as people who aren't creative; each of us has the desire and the capability to create and to enhance. Growing a garden creates life, feeds people, and beautifies the environment. Putting up a building requires tremendous skill and the ability to come up with creative solutions to problems. Raising children creates life, educates, and empowers. Helping to build a movement creates hope. Playing charades creates laughter and community.

Creative involvement is a basic need. Would you like to sing in a choir at your church? Join your community garden? Build a dollhouse or make models? Take a drawing or writing or cooking class at your community college? Learn a musical instrument? Read? (Reading is creative because you have to form images in your mind of what you're reading; this image-making is missing when we watch a screen.)

And notice ways in which you are already being creative, including activities that you may not have thought of as being in that category.

Community

We have been creatures of community for hundreds of thousands of years. Our security comes from knowing that other people care what happens to us, that they will go to great lengths to keep us well. We crave the connection that comes from shared concerns, collective plans, common goals. We want to be spokes in a wheel. Look for ways to build community into your life.

Even in our scattered times, community abides. Networks of friends form loosely-knit societies that revolve around cook-outs, outings to the beach, marriages and funerals. Faith communities bring their members together to rejoice in shared values and visions and to watch out for each other. Charitable and political organizations attract individuals with concern and commitment who want to share a mission. The best workplaces have atmospheres of caring and common purpose.

Some communities exist for only a few days or even a few hours. As a loved one passes away, a group of friends and family spend a series of days crying together, bringing food to each other's houses, coordinating turns at the hospital, and planning for the memorial service. Survivors of natural disasters attempt to take care of everyone, combining efforts and sharing what resources they have. A neighborhood is unified to stop a commercial development or a toxic-waste facility. Weddings, funerals, retirement parties, births: these commemorations act like crystals, drawing surrounding people into a caring society.

Children hunger for community. You never hear a young one say, "I'm tired of having so many people around" (unless the child is getting ignored). Notice that even young children keep mental track of quite a number of people, referring to them frequently and expressing a desire to see them. Children crave a regular connection to many more people than are contained in a nuclear family.

An awareness of the power of community is what motivates the building of the Peak Living Network. When we combine caring community with extensive knowledge about how to heal, we have an unstoppable force.

Exercise and Nutrition

We need to take care of our bodies in order to be well *emotionally*. One of the first things a therapist should ask a client is, "What have you been eating lately and what has your physical activity been like?" Research finds that regular exercise is more effective in relieving depression *than even the most effective anti-depressant medication*; it's unethical for a doctor to put you on drugs before first putting you on exercise.

When we're in bad shape emotionally we often cope with our feelings by eating badly and we lose our motivation to get exercise, creating a nasty feedback loop. These are areas we need to attend to as part of a larger strategy to get emotionally well.

An Equal and Effective Voice

We have the absolute human right to have our homes, communities, and workplaces fully and equitably controlled by the people who live and work in them. We need our full share of the influence over every decision that affects us and affects the other living things we care about. But modern societies could scarcely be farther from honoring these rights; workplaces are controlled by the people who own them, governments are run by a tiny percentage of people in the wealthy class, families are typically under the rule of one male.

As part of improving our mental health we need to join with others to stand up against authoritarianism in our homes, workplaces, communities, and societies. Reclaiming our say is a basic need.

Natural Beauty

Disconnection from the natural world breeds sadness. Our inner emptinesses are not just about the shortage of human contact but also about the ways in which we've been pulled apart from the other forms of life with which we share the planet. When it's impossible to live close to nature—an outcome that never should have been allowed to happen in the first place—we need at least to know that the wild places *are there,* to be able to picture them in our minds and dream of them. We all lose in our mental health when natural beauty is paved over.

Access to nature is increasingly impeded, but we can find avenues. Community gardens, found even in the hearts of urban environments, give residents a way to interact with living things and feel ecological connection. Plants in the house and flowers in the yard feed the soul in their simple way. Photographs and posters of spectacular outdoor settings enliven a house. Driving to the ocean or to a state park to take a walk on the weekend gives us a chance to soak up the beauty and wonder of creation. Seek to rebuild your natural bond with the glory of the natural world.

Connection to All That Is

Our need for connection is a set of concentric circles. The innermost ring is the desire for emotional intimacy with ourselves and our loved ones. The next circle outward is the need to be an integral part of a larger community. The third circle takes us to the longing for connection to all people and all living things.

The last, outermost ring is our craving to belong to *everything that exists.* It is the realm of religion and spirituality, of meditation and contemplation. It is made up of whatever activities, gatherings, or beliefs make you feel one with all of creation.

Some people find a joyous home away from home in a religious community or meditation circle. Other people say, "I believe in love," or even, "I believe in science." The particular path is not the issue; what matters is that you find a place or a practice that brings you close to those things that matter most to you, to your deepest values and your most ardent loves, and ultimately to everything.

Spiritual connection should be joyful. If your services or prayers focus on obedience to authority, condemning non-believers, or rituals that feel empty to you, your soul will hunger. You may need, openly or secretly, to seek out a new spiritual community, or a special place to sit with a view, or a book of meditations, or a photograph of Mount Everest. Seek a path that brings you to that delicious moment of oneness.

As long as we live we need to return periodically to the questions at the core of our being:

What are my most cherished and deepest beliefs?

What do I most love with all my heart?

What do I hold to be the highest truths?

What do I find most beautiful?

What is the place or experience that makes me feel most at peace and most at one?

If you have suffered mistreatment in the name of religion or spirituality, as many people have, there's no need to use words or concepts that were used to hurt you. Pursue deep and wide connection using the terminology and beliefs *that work for you.* You're related to everything that exists, and you have the right to revel in that.

A Chance to Heal

Finally, we need chances for our emotional healing processes to work as they were designed to do. Life inevitably involves emotional injury; even in a world that was free of oppression we would still experience the loss of loved ones, natural disasters, physical injuries (which take their emotional toll), and some injustices. We will always need our emotional releases and other healing processes keep us whole and intact.

———————————

Naturally you can't address all these needs at once. Progress will come in increments. Start where you can, valuing the importance of each effort however small. Each improvement you make in finding what you need will give you strength for the next step. The better you get your needs met, the more deeply your healing processes will function. In turn, the more you heal, the more clarity you'll get about how to find what you need. You'll feel your life getting richer almost immediately, with many more gains to come.

Key Points to Remember:

- We all meet our needs in different ways, but the core needs that are driving us are the same for everyone.

- Some things that we feel like we need (like power or material possessions or substances) are actually symptoms of our wounds rather than being true needs.

- Finding ways to get our needs met better supports our healing, and healing helps us get more successful at finding ways to meet our needs. The two feed each other beautifully.

Part Four

Taking on the World

Chapter Eighteen

Overcoming Oppression and Internalized Oppression

As self-help book after self-help book analyzes our wounds, habits, and dysfunctional families, they fail to say anything about the *deepest sources* of our emotional injuries. The devastating force I'm referring to is *oppression*: the way in which societies take away people's rights group by group and target those people for mistreatment. This subject still seems to be on the "don't mention it" list.

Everyone has endured oppression. We haven't all endured it equally, but we've all suffered it enough that the pain we carry inside us is actually about oppression more than anything else.

The Oppression That Misses No One

One form of oppression is so nearly universal and socially accepted that few people question it: *the oppression of children.*

Contempt for children is so widespread that most adults have no awareness of their own attitudes; in fact, they laugh if you point out the degradation that's taking place. "But that's just the way kids are," they say. The more something is present everywhere you look, the harder it can be to see it.

Another reason for the invisibility of the oppression of children is that everyone escapes it eventually, and moreover we escape it *very gradually*. That's why we barely remember what it was like; it faded away a tiny piece at a time as we got older. When we were ten years old and still felt everyone looking down on us, we'd already started to feel superior to six-year-olds. When we were twelve or fourteen it started getting harder for adults to hit or frighten us. At some point our opinions started to carry a little weight, and then a little more. The pain and injustice faded into forgetfulness like a fog.

Children know that the way they're being treated is not right, but they get hurt even worse if they dare say so; so over time they gradually forget their outrage. Or, more accurately, they learn to channel their outrage toward each other, toward people who don't deserve it, or toward a path to become "bad kids."

I have a distinct memory at nine or ten years old of thinking to myself one day, "I wonder if children have rights, too." Two more thoughts quickly followed: first, that I was being ridiculous and, second, that everyone else would also think so. As a result, I never told anyone.

Chapter 2 examined the wrongs that children are *routinely* subjected to, including:

- *Violence.* Children have no legal right to live free of physical assault. In fact, there are special terms for assaulting children, such as "spanking," "physical discipline," and "a little swat on the behind" to make it all sound okay.

- *Contempt.* Children are treated as if they're stupid. Adults tend to put on a special "I'm talking to a child" voice, as if addressing idiots.

- *Silencing.* Children are given almost no say over their lives, and when they attempt to protest injustices, adults use intimidation to shut them up.

- *Invasion.* The breaking of children's physical and sexual boundaries is rampant, and doesn't become illegal until it reaches extreme forms.

- *Portrayed negatively.* Children are regarded as unreasonable, selfish, uncooperative, lacking in judgment, or "just wanting attention." They live in this atmosphere of negativity about their entire group.

- *Imprisoned indoors.* Schooling, urbanization, and other factors have condemned children to spend the bulk of their lives indoors and away from the places and activities they most cherish. They are required to sit still, which is unnatural for children, and are subjected to torturous boredom.

- *Their needs and feelings ignored.* The love, caretaking, and valuing that children are *not* given is in many ways as harmful as the overt mistreatment they are subjected to.

The above list is just what happens *routinely* to kids. Beyond this we have the realm of child labor, sex trafficking, sadistic cruelty, and more.

Long ago a tribal leader on the North American continent observed that the Europeans "seem to hate their children." There were documented cases of white kids running away to live with tribes, where children were treated with kindness and respect; and of cases where those children were "rescued from the savages" but ran back to the tribe the first chance they got.

Our First Experience of Inferiority

The experience of children points to the most crushing aspect of oppression (short of outright slavery and violence): being made to feel that, just because of the group that you're in, you are inherently less. You're less valuable, less intelligent, and less human, and therefore not worthy of being taken seriously. The pain of being viewed in this way is sharpened when you see that view reinforced wherever you go: in movies and television, in jokes and sayings, and in how you see your people being treated. You're constantly reminded that you're *inferior*.

Children were once your people. (Perhaps they still are). You carry a weight of pain about wrongs you saw done to other kids, not just what happened to you.

Central Characteristics of Oppression

Oppression is about *power* and *control*. As hurtful as individual prejudice and discrimination are, there are other forces that have a much greater impact; namely, the way in which powerful groups in society use policies, punishments, and media to bully other groups. So while it's unquestionably terrible for a landlord to deny a rental to a family because they're dark-skinned, that damage pales compared to what happens when government officials decide to pursue policies designed to lead to mass incarceration of people of color. (See the documentary "13" if you haven't already.)

We need to attend to oppression at both levels; at the micro level of overcoming bigoted attitudes and individual acts of discrimination, and at the macro level of dismantling powerful social systems.

Dynamics Common to All Systems of Oppression:

- The use of violence and intimidation, including the threat of violence, starvation and the threat of starvation, and incarceration

- Sexual violence and boundary invasion toward many members of the target group

- Vastly unfair distribution of wealth and other desirable elements of life, including access to leisure time, open space, health care, healthful food, and water

- The target group being characterized as inherently inferior—less intelligent, less logical, less honest, less deep, and less competent

- The pervasive telling of lies about that group, including the burying of the group's history and the twisting of current events to make the group look bad

- Power and control—the taking away of the group's rights, freedom, and say

- Silencing and retaliation for efforts by the group to name the wrongs being done to them

- Fostering the group's dependence on the powerful group, including sabotaging any progress toward independence

- Making it hard for members of the group to find empowering information (such as barring prisoners from receiving books and magazines that explain prisoners' legal rights)

- Taking children away from parents for unjustifiable reasons (selling slaves, imprisoning tribal children in "boarding schools," taking children by child protective systems for racist or classist reasons disguised as mercy)

Dynamics Common to Most Systems of Oppression:

- Exploitation of the group's labor—slavery, unpaid and underpaid work, dangerous working conditions, long hours, little vacation, and no say over anything significant during the workday

- Exploitation and theft of the group's resources—taking away their land, hunting grounds, and fishing grounds; taking water sources and waterways; polluting the group's land, water, and air

Nothing can justify these actions, yet we're faced daily with attempts to do so. I can remember by age five being exposed to images and stories that taught me that tribal people were headhunters, had limited intelligence, and stood in the way of "progress" due to their superstitions. These portrayals served to mask the destruction of tribal lives and all that they held sacred.

The Powerful vs. Everyone Else

For the past few thousand years smaller and smaller groups of people have gradually been taking over all societies. Most people in our time have no say over the key decisions that get made at national and regional levels; all the significant power is in the hands of a tiny percentage of extremely wealthy and influential people.

Most of the rest of us have to work for the wealthy class to make a living. That class controls most of our work places and determines how the economy functions. We are required to work so much that there's little time for anything else, and we get just a few weeks off each year. We get little or no say over how the workplace functions, whom we work with, and what our workplace produces; that's all up to the bosses.

Rule by the wealthy class is so pervasive that it becomes hard for people to see how wrong it is; it's just "life." Our jobs make us tired, stressed, and angry, and we're plagued with sadness about the things we don't get to do because we're working so much. And we take a lot of that pain out on each other and on ourselves.

The proper name for this is class *oppression* or *classism*; a few people get the power and the luxuries while everyone else does the hard work.

There are better jobs and worse jobs, better neighborhoods and worse neighborhoods, better schools and worse schools. But these distinctions serve to hide what's really going on, which is that we're all losing our quality of life.

The Oppression of Women

When you hear the word "worker," what image comes to your mind? Most likely it was a man. But according to UN statistics, women do *70%* of the world's labor. This is a huge imbalance, and it illustrates how we're taught to see the world upside down. The main reason sexism exists is to make women do way more than their share of the work.

At the same time, sexism is about much more than just labor, involving:

- the exploitation of women's sexuality.
- the silencing of women's thinking.

- the control and intimidation of women through male violence.

- the pervasive negative portrayals of females in media.

When people hear the word "sexism," they tend to think only of sex-role stereotyping, such as not letting boys play with dolls and telling girls not to get dirty. When we look only at this dynamic, we can mistakenly believe that sexism hurts females and males roughly equally. But sex-role stereotyping is one tiny piece of a vast oppressive system that targets females.

I explore these concepts in greater depth in my article, "Talking Man to Man About Sexism," which you can read at PeakLivingNetwork.org. That article (which isn't just for men) also recommends other readings about gender oppression.

How Men Can Be Allies to Women's Healing

If you're male, you may wonder, "How can I best be a good support to the females in my life?" The top priority is to listen well when women tell what things have been like for them, taking it all in without getting defensive. Consider it a gift—and a vote of confidence—that a woman is speaking angrily to you; it means she thinks you're capable of hearing. *Don't* respond with stuff about how hard it is to be a man; if you shift the discussion to your own experience you'll never understand what hers has been.

The next priorities are:

1) Support women's leadership by offering encouragement, respect, financing, space to lead, and childcare

2) Do the concrete work we tend to avoid (clean up, give good attention to children, change diapers, make food, and more)

Be attentive to who's doing the talking, who's making the decisions, who's cleaning the room after meetings, whose opinions are being given weight. Don't slip into that tone of voice that conveys the message, "I'm now going to explain the *right* answer to you," including starting statements with, "What you have to understand is…" We aren't the ultimate authority.

Oppression Based on Race

I am writing this book during a surge of protest in the United States against the murder of people of color by police officers. Of the 147 unarmed people killed by police during 2017, 82 were black or Hispanic.[1] This is just one example of the myriad forms of intimidation that are a common aspect of life for people of color in the United States.

The presence of people of African descent on this continent is a product of the slave trade, which led to the deaths of *50 million* Africans. Prior to the African tragedy, the North American and South American continents had already been ravaged by white invaders in a similar way.

Although many people believe that racism in the U.S. was largely overcome during the 1960's, the reality is that people of color are in a worse position, economically and otherwise, in our era. The incarceration of black men has *quintupled*. The official stealing of tribal lands continues apace. Racism against Muslims is skyrocketing. The 1960's uprising against racism was indeed powerful, inspiring, and important; but oppressive systems keep reinventing themselves, and thus the need to fight back continues.

The Peak Living Network exists to be a force for heal-

[1] www.theroot.com/heres-how-many-people-police-killed-in-2017-1821706614

ing in the world. Toward that end, we all need to expand our ability to listen—to *really* listen—to people who decide to tell the truth about the oppression that they, and their people, have endured. White people need to not turn defensive when people of color describe the realities of their lives, and instead *hear* and *digest* what's being expressed. Remember, people don't bother telling you the truth unless they have hope that you will be able to take it in.

Facing the Realities of Oppression Is Crucial to Healing

It can feel like a heavy load to think seriously about oppression. However, the load actually gets *lighter*, not heavier, when we move bravely into these issues. As you start to digest the reality of what oppression has meant in your own life, and in the lives of people you care about, you'll find that you begin to feel more hopeful and powerful, not less so. And your healing will be enhanced.

The failure to examine and address the role that systematic oppression plays in our emotional injuries is one of the central reasons why current popular approaches to healing and recovery are not working well.

Oppression Takes Many Forms

Any time an identifiable group of people systematically get their rights taken away from them by a more powerful group in the society that views them as inferior, oppression is taking place. These dynamics cause many of our deepest hurts and keep us divided against each other.

- *Homophobia* or *heterosexism* is the oppression of lesbians and gay men, people who form their primary love relationships with members of their own sex. In addition to the direct damage done by homophobia, it is used as a weapon to force women and men to play their stereotypical roles in society; for example, women who choose to live independently may get labeled "lesbian," and men who refuse to take on the toxic aspects of masculinity may be taunted as gay.

- *Imperialism* is the exploitation of the labor and resources of an entire people or nation. The powerful countries of the world have grown their wealth by invading other countries, terrorizing the residents, and taking control, while always claiming to be there to help.

- *Antisemitism* is the targeting of Jews. It not only has obvious profound historical significance through the Nazi genocide, but remains a more powerful dynamic today than most people realize. The scapegoating of Jews has been used for many centuries by powerful ruling groups. It is on the rise again.

- *Ageism* is the oppression of older people. Older people are disrespected in myriad ways, and their portrayal in media is often negative and disrespectful. Old people get labeled as "out of touch" and "unable to adapt to change," rather than being viewed as a critical source of wisdom, which was their traditional role.

- *Authoritarianism* is the oppression of people by institutions that they are part of, most commonly the countries they live in. Governments, police forces (both public and private), and militaries play important roles at various times in stifling dissent and keeping people intimidated.

Internalized Oppression

Oppression doesn't just function against us on the outside: it crawls inside of us, distorting our view of ourselves. We are conditioned to hate ourselves and our bodies, to dislike other members of our own group, and to buy into the belief that what was done to us was our own fault. Children feel that if they could just be smarter, better-behaved, or better-looking, then bad things wouldn't happen to them. Working people are made to feel that if they just worked harder, got a better education, and cared more about the company (ugh), they would move up the ladder and have more possessions and freedom.

This inner harm causes us to *identify with* our oppressors and adopt their beliefs, trying to get in good with them and modeling ourselves after their ways of living. Children long to be adults, or at least one of the "big kids." Working people admire the rich and devour their stories in the media. Members of the wealthy class don't just think they're better, they succeed in getting us to believe it too.

One impact of internalized oppression is that it turns us against each other; for example, we may distance ourselves from members of our own group to show that we "aren't like the others." Our internal images of ourselves are shaped by media and societal portrayals of groups that we belong to, leading us to blame ourselves and each other for our hardships.

Healing from oppression therefore needs to include processing the ways we've been turned against ourselves—including our bodies—and turned against our own people.

Drawing Some Threads Together

The naming of oppression is powerful in helping us to:

- recognize and digest what has been done to us and to our people.

- heal the wounds that systemic mistreatment has caused us.

- find ways to fight for our rights and overthrow oppressive systems.

The targets of oppression—which means all of us, since everyone has to pass through the gauntlet of childhood—carry the pain of those experiences. We hurt for what was done to us and for what was done to our entire people. We hurt about cruelty that we had to witness and were forbidden to intervene against. We hurt from watching our children targeted. Perhaps most deeply of all, we hurt from seeing the society justify and ignore the harm.

Resistance to Oppression Springs Eternal

Amidst all this there remains a place deep inside us that hasn't given up, where we long to live a life free of oppression, in a free world.

Oppressed people are not just collections of wounds. Inside they have resilience, strength, and wisdom. They keep rising again to fight once more for their rights. The oppressed will never give up.

There is so much power to be found in recovering our personal histories of resistance to oppression. That power grows even more when we also learn the history of our people's resistance, going back hundreds or thousands of years. Resistance continues today far more than we hear about. Our liberation movements efforts grow stronger when we have the inspiration and wisdom that comes from knowing our pasts.

You have a personal history of resisting oppression, both for yourself and other people. You may have forgotten important parts of that history, which began with how upset you were when you first became aware of injustice. *Hating oppression as a young child was your first act of resistance.* Start remembering how you fought, both visibly and silently, not to go along with it. You absolutely did, for as long as you could.

Key Points to Remember:

- Not only is healing a collective process, *injury* is largely a collective process. Most of what has hurt us the worst was happening to countless others at the same time.

- "Dysfunctional families" are a product of even deeper wrongs in our society.

- You have fought against oppression, whether you remember doing so or not.

- Oppression is the most pervasive — yet least discussed — cause of our emotional wounds.

- Oppression becomes internalized, eating away at us from inside until we get the chance to heal.

- We can talk about it. And we can work together to dismantle it.

Chapter Nineteen

Building a World That Works for Everyone

A widespread myth about emotional healing goes like this:

"You have to get your own self together before you can help anyone else. You have to change yourself before you can change the world."

This myth becomes a voice in our heads saying,

"I'm not ready to take on the burdens of the world and justice. I have to focus on myself."

These views are actually working against our recovery. Here's why:

1. Our Deepest Wounds Are Rooted in Powerlessness

Underlying our worst experiences is the bitter fact that we couldn't make them stop. Each deep injury therefore contains another injury within it, the excruciating experience of powerlessness.

One of the central insights of the Peak Living Network approach is that emotional recovery moves very slowly unless we can find examples in our present lives that run *counter* to the dynamics of the old injury. For deep healing of our old experiences of loneliness and isolation, we first need to build close connections with people today. For healing from danger and invasion, we first need to find a safe place today. To heal from the emotional effects of past starvation, we first need enough to eat today.

So if we're wanting to heal from past powerlessness and injustice, *we first need examples today of ways in which we're acting powerfully to pursue what's right.*

We naturally face challenges in this process. For example, most of us go through periods when we feel too broken to reach out to new people; at these times we feel like we have to do a lot of healing *first,* and then try to build new love and friendship into our lives. But if we can't heal well until we reach out, and we can't reach out until we heal, where do we start?

The only effective answer is to do them both at the same time. Each day some healing time, each day some powerful action. We can't wait until we feel ready to act powerfully; if we wait, that day never comes.

2. Social Injustice Underlies Most Experiences of Powerlessness

Our personal experiences have not been entirely personal; they are actually connected to destructive things that were happening to lots and lots of people like us, as we explored in the previous chapter. Hence the saying, "The personal is political."

Given that we're all carrying the aftereffects of injustice, where do we look for the personal counterexamples that will fuel our healing? We find them when we're involved in fighting against injustice in the present, building a world that works for everyone.

Changing the World Isn't What You Think It Is

1. It Isn't Candidates and Voting

When people say, "I'm not interested in politics," they're usually referring to electoral politics—senators, representatives, presidents. But when I talk about "politics," I'm talking in much broader terms. I'm referring to *every decision and choice that gets made that affects large numbers of people or the natural environment.*

And when I use the terms "social justice" and "social change" I'm talking about *efforts to return decision-making power to its rightful owners—meaning the people who are affected by a decision or a policy.*

In today's world, most decisions that govern the quality of our lives are made far away, and we have almost no say over them. A society that was based on the principle that everyone should have equal decision-making input would look *nothing* like modern countries.

So how do we reclaim our right to govern our own lives? Since efforts to make changes by voting tend to lead to frustration, we need to determine strategies that genuinely build our collective power (see the box on page 276).

2. It Isn't Marching, Chanting, and Carrying Signs

Well, except when you want it to be.

The common image of activism is that it's all about going to meetings and wearing buttons, carried out by radicals who are into using violence. Activists are viewed as overly serious people trying to save the world by pushing for extreme responses when instead "they should just learn to get along."

As modern citizens, our real say comes through:

- Forming collective organizations to fight for our rights

- Taking control of our own neighborhoods, towns, and school systems, fighting for local autonomy

- Boycotts and other mass refusals to cooperate (such as mass refusals to register for the draft, or mass refusals by students to take standardized tests)

- Strikes, sick-outs, sit-downs, work stoppages

- Truth-telling through writing, art, theater, film, and other avenues for publicly expressing our views

- Demonstrations, pickets, rallies, marches, vigils

- Blockades, occupations, and other forms of civil disobedience and direct action

- Forming local food systems, currencies, and energy distribution systems to reduce the power of central authorities; developing an independent local economy; creating grassroots systems to address community mental health, support the arts, and prepare for emergencies

The reality of social change looks nothing like these images. Let's begin by redefining our terms:

Activist: A person who devotes time and mental energy to taking stands against injustice and environmental destruction, striving to join with others in common efforts to build a healthier world

Activism: Concerted efforts, carried out in communication and cooperation with other people, that challenge the behavior of powerful institutions and seek to return power to its rightful owners (the people who are affected by the decisions)

You may already be an activist without realizing it. If you believe the world should work differently, and you attempt to use your influence to bring that about, that's activism.

Activists are not one kind of person. They are as likely to be humorous as serious, playful as overworking, well-liked as irritating, skillful communicators as chanters of slogans. We don't look anything like the media's stereotyped images. Most activists don't consider themselves radicals, but those who do are almost all opposed to the use of violence.

Charity vs. Justice

Catholic Archbishop Dom Helder Camara is known worldwide for saying:

"When I give food to hungry people, they call me a saint; when I ask why the people are hungry, they call me a communist."

Charity and activism are two different things. Charity works to meet the needs that our social systems fail to meet. Activism strives to change our social systems so that they properly meet people's needs (and the needs of the earth). Neither is more important than the other; both are essential.

As you work to make a difference in the world, look both at ways to provide more to people in need and at ways to speak out more, questioning why they're having to live in those conditions in the first place. The line between charity and activism becomes blurred — in a good way — when providers of assistance encourage people to examine the wider causes of their difficulties. For example, if I provide drug treatment in a poor neighborhood, I can take my work to a more powerful level by also starting discussions about the policies that lead our communities to be riddled with drugs.

Finding the Best Role for Yourself

Instead of thinking, "I'm not the kind of person who takes on the world," proceed on the assumption that you just haven't found your place within that effort yet. Consider these important roles:

- speaking to friends and relatives about injustice and how to address it, and encouraging them to get involved

- writing about your beliefs and sharing what you've written

- bringing social justice concerns into your creative work (art, dance, theater, music)

- supporting other activists (listening to them and encouraging them, providing child care, making food, bailing them out of jail after political arrests)

- doing charitable work and bringing a social justice view to that work (we might call it "feeding hungry people while also asking why the people are hungry")

- creating new organizations and movements, raising new issues

- showing up for social justice and environmental events

- helping to unionize your workplace or getting more involved with your union if you already have one

- countless other possibilities (see the boxed section a few pages back)

You can contribute to world-changing efforts in a way that's right for you. When we feel that we're helping build a world where people won't get injured in the ways that we were, our hearts gain strength for recovery.

If your gut tells you strongly that this the wrong time for you to get involved in justice efforts, maybe that's true. But consider giving it one good effort to be sure. If it turns out that this really isn't the moment, there will be a time later when it is.

It's important to take care of your well-being while you take on the world. Attend to these elements:

1) Be involved in an issue or cause that moves you.

Don't choose a particular issue out of a sense of obligation. Instead, work on something that energizes and inspires you. Try to keep drawing your motivation from your heart; that's what will be most valuable to the world and best further your own healing.

2) Don't take on too much.

Human suffering is an urgent matter. But we don't help the world much if we destroy our health or undermine our enjoyment of life. Social action should feed and strengthen us, not drain or isolate us.

3) Avoid toxic people.

Work with people whom you enjoy working with and look forward to seeing. At times it may be worth switching organizations or issues in order to feel fed and supported by the people you're around. Try to resolve conflicts, but notice when these efforts take too much of a toll on you; at that point, take some distance and find people to collaborate with who feed your soul.

4) Set goals for success.

Make sure you have short-term goals, not just long-term ones, and that they are reasonable ones. Put value on relationship-building, public education, spreading leadership skills, and other measurable steps; it's important to notice and celebrate what we're accomplishing, whether or not we succeed in the big fight that is our goal.

5) Build support, make time for co-counseling, and keep healing.

Emotional healing and social activism support each other. Don't sacrifice one to the other.

People who are involved in social justice efforts can benefit from developing greater awareness of emotional wounds and healing processes. And those involved in healing and spiritual work can benefit through greater awareness of injustice and environmental harm. Bringing these two ends toward each other is of utmost urgency in today's world.

See Yourself and Others As Leaders

There is no such thing as "the leader type" and "the follower type." We all need to develop leadership skills in the areas of our lives where we have the most to offer.

A good leader is not someone who tells other people what to do, nor is it someone who believes that their opinions and strategies are superior. When I ask you to see yourself as a leader I mean that I want you to:

- Know that you can help move efforts forward.

- Think about what's good for the whole group.

- Take initiative without waiting for someone's permission (while also honoring group process and agreements).

- See yourself as someone who can start new efforts or projects when you see a need.

- Develop your skills in writing, speaking, and facilitating.

- Read about the issue that calls to you; deepen your knowledge and analysis.

- Be prepared to take a stand that may be unpopular in your society or even in your own social circle; stand up for what you really think.

A good leader also attempts to spread power, not accumulate it, through efforts to:

- Notice when someone isn't being heard—even if it's someone you disagree with yourself—and make sure that their perspective is not silenced or skipped over.

- Notice people who demonstrate potential leadership skills; encourage them to be confident, speak up, and take initiatives.

- Encourage and support people toward leadership who are underrepresented in those roles, including women, people of color, and people raised working class; supporting other leaders is a form of leadership.

- Offer opportunities for people to be trained in leadership skills, including group facilitation, media skills, and public speaking.

Remembering a Key Healing Concept

Our healing flows best when we build elements into our current lives that run sharply counter to the injuries we carry. If we grew up isolated, it's extra important to build close relationships today. If we grew up being criticized, we have extra need today for an environment that is supportive and encouraging. If we grew up around threats, we need super safe places today. These counterweights to our past distresses don't bring healing by themselves, but they create the *context* in which healing, including deep emotional release, best progresses. Since our deepest wounds come from experiences of injustice, our healing accelerates when we can see ourselves confronting injustices, both in our own lives and in our wider world.

Key Points to Remember:

- It doesn't work well to focus on healing today and changing the world tomorrow. The two processes both go better when they're interwoven.

- Reflect on the question of what imprint you want to leave on the world. We need you to share your gifts.

- Reclaiming your power as an individual is connected to reclaiming your power as part of a larger group. Personal power is linked to *collective* power, which brings forth the most significant improvements in our lives.

Chapter Twenty

Living in Love and Awareness

I am inviting you on a healing journey. Bring with you the aching wounds in your heart, the losses, the betrayals, and the empty spaces. Think of yourself as heading to a grand and colorful plaza, where you and I and many others will be meeting to lay out our stories like bruised but beautiful fruit. Each heartrending account of courage and triumph, of alienation and despair, of hope almost lost, will float on the breeze to loving ears, making history. We will roar and tremble and weep. Lost energy will flow inside of us. Afterwards we'll each go home to sleep deeply and warmly, the arms of the world wrapped tightly around us.

I am inviting you to renewal. The potential for human healing is never extinguished until the literal life flies from the body. Until that moment, life can always begin anew.

I am inviting you to reawaken your dreams. They still dwell within you somewhere, waiting for you to come back for them. You may occasionally experience flashes where life feels completely different, perhaps brought on by a special laugh with a favorite person, evening colors in the sky, or an aroma in the air — or sometimes for no reason that you can discern. These are glimpses of what's possible; keep them incubating and they'll grow.

At the same time, I invite you to forget about "succeeding," trying to live up to *other people's expectations* for you. Instead, pursue what you really want, focusing on what will feed your soul.

I am inviting you to hope. There is a way out. There's a way out of loneliness and isolation. There's a way out of abuse and degradation. There's a way out of slavery, of war, of the destruction of all that's beautiful. We can do what must be done.

I am inviting you back to yourself. You're still all there.

Leaning Into Love

Love is our purpose. The reason we struggle with the question, "What is the meaning of life?" is that we live in a disconnected world. If we spent our days steeped in each other's love, each of us doing work that we knew treated the earth and its inhabitants in a loving way, if we got to love this beautiful world without worrying about its future health, the meaning of life would be self-evident. Our days would feel so significant that it would never occur to us to question the meaning of life.

Human healing has love as both cause and effect. The more we get to feel and express our love for others, the more our pain eases and shifts. The more we feel other people valuing and appreciating us, the more our internal barriers crumble and purifying tears flow. Love leads to healing.

But it's equally true that healing leads to love. When we get a chance to free ourselves of the effects of our injuries, when the accumulated pain of tragedies and outrages gets the chance to run like rivers out of us, we emerge wiping our tears away and smiling warmly on the people we see.

The store clerk becomes someone to have fun with instead of an obstacle to hurry past. The stranger on the street becomes someone whose eyes we look into, at least briefly, and wonder about their story. We start wanting to spread a blanket out on the grass and share a meal. The more we heal, the more we find that loving other people is just the natural way to live.

Live each day breaking down the barriers to loving everyone you meet. Tell people what you notice and appreciate about them. Don't hold back the words 'I love you," but also don't parrot them as an obligation, as in, "Love you, 'bye." Put your heart in it, feel it when you say it.

Take risks to love. Risk rejection, risk annoyance, risk the person pulling away because your love scares them. Risk looking silly. *Holding back carries a far greater risk.*

When you're with children, spend less time molding and improving them and more time just letting them be who they are, showering them with love and acceptance.

Keep working through barriers to safe, appropriate physical affection with those you care about. Walk with your arm inside of another person's arm, brush someone's hair, rub a friend's feet, hold your healing partner while he or she laughs or cries or rests.

Love awarely, love skillfully. Love is an art form, especially in a wounded world.

Love will poke you where you need to heal. When love aches and burns, as it sometimes will, don't pull away; instead, let it guide you to the places where you need to rub salve on your soul, where the tears need to flow, where you need to hear—or write—a piece of music. Heal, heal, heal.

Let's start really noticing the hearts we're holding and hold them well. Keep an eye out for my heart, and I'll be watching out for yours.

Our Inherent Nature

Human beings are not blank slates, easily molded by the environment. We are deeply, inherently good. We want to be close to people, we want to have fun, we want to work together. It takes an avalanche of terrible experiences to harden us, to make us stop believing in our species, to make us attack each other. We kick and scream for as long as we can before we start to give up the best parts of ourselves.

Think about the babies you've known. Did you ever meet a baby that was hostile from the start? Who didn't like to be held? Who tried to figure out how to hurt people? Who was happier alone than accompanied? Who didn't trust people? Babies expect the world to be good to them; they're shocked if it isn't. They're ready for anyone who wants to hold them or play with them. They will gaze adoringly at anyone who is kind to them and takes the time to connect; they're open to the world. They get upset if anyone else is upset. *There is simply no such thing as a bad baby.*

And we were all babies once.

Another way we can tell that people are intrinsically good is by watching what happens as they heal. No one experiences deep healing and then moves in the direction of violence and selfishness. Everyone who gets that sweet taste of recovery craves more kindness and more cooperation in their lives. Healing reveals the profound truth of who we are.

In fact, when you experience deep healing you come to feel more and more determined that no one, *no one*, is to be left behind. It's not that you can be everyone's personal rescuer—you can't, and it isn't healthful to try—but you *can* rescue a few, and the rest of us can each rescue a few— even as we ourselves are being rescued. Together we can get ourselves and everyone else to dry land.

Even people that for now we have to stay well away from, because they are toxic to us, we hope to return for some day; when we collectively have the knowledge and resources to stop their destructiveness and give them the unique help they need.

No one truly wants power over other people, no one truly wants to do harm. Deep inside of everyone there is something that predated deep traumatic injury and societally-conditioned hostility; a being who wants to live in community and harmony, who wants a world that works for everyone.

Achieving Fluidity

Just as emotional injury leads us to become rigid and pattern-driven, emotional healing carries us toward greater and greater flexibility. Remember for a moment a time when your body released and become fluid, the aches and stiffness disappearing for a little while. Perhaps it was brought on by soaking in a hot bath or shower, a great massage, an unusually comfortable bed, or a great night of dancing. We want that same experience in our inner world, where the fears and anxieties subside, the compulsions stop pushing us around, we stop steeling ourselves against heartbreak or rejection. We can achieve moments of inner fluidity, and then more of them, and still more, until they become the norm.

The more flexible we become, the more everything starts to seem possible. We take leaps we never thought we could take, we stop desperately groping for our morning coffee, we become close with someone we thought we could never be friends with, we find creative and elegant solutions to problems we considered insoluble. Our literal dreams may change—perhaps we don't dream of being astronauts or ballet dancers anymore—but the craving for a truly fulfilling life starts to be attainable.

Rigidity tells us that we have to either be wishy-washy or closed minded, that those are the only choices. Flexibility tells us that there's a third way, where we fight like hell for what we believe in today yet remain open to modifying our beliefs tomorrow as we grow and learn.

Balance, Balance, Balance

Allow balance to become the norm in your life. We make our days rich in the present, while also continuing to heal from the past, by:

- balancing time for emotional healing with time spent celebrating successes and loving life today.

- balancing efforts to take care of ourselves with action to build a humane world.

- balancing meeting our own needs with expanding the support we offer to those we care about.

- balancing acceptance of things as they are with decisive action to improve them.

- balancing deep, serene rest with courageous and tireless work and adventure.

- balancing excitement and tenacity about our beliefs with flexibility and open-mindedness.

- balancing independent initiative with the building of a wide base of support and assistance.

- balancing inner reflection and solitude with deep, un-fettered connections to other people.

These balancing acts contain the essence of loving, thinking, and living flexibly.

Ordinary Living

The principles I've shared are ordinary qualities of human life. It has to become completely normal for someone to be crying hard on the bus, and none of the other passengers get uncomfortable or assume that there's a crisis. No one starts calling her "depressed" because she's grieving. A couple of people just calmly sit near her and offer to take her hand.

Meetings, whether at work or not, need to start routinely breaking for a few minutes for people to split time in pairs, getting support and attending to what they're feeling. Everyone's opinions needs to be heard and their preferences given weight.

We have to start really listening to each other and truly hearing. We need to hear what children and old people are trying to tell us, along with the voices of everyone else who has been pushed to the sides.

All of these ways of being need to become commonplace, no longer seeming special.

————————

Each of us is a miracle, a triumph, no matter how defeated we feel some days or some years. You in particular have so much to be proud of, so much that you've done well in the face of adversity. And the strengths you have are just beginning to flourish. The future holds so much more for you: more joy, more closeness, more justice.

Please join me on the journey into healing. The departure gate is open and everyone is invited. The trip will be exhilarating, painful, inspiring, frightening—and joyous. It's the journey back into life itself, which we've lost along our weary paths. I hope to see you there.

Appendix

My Story

I grew up primarily in the Northeastern United States, the youngest of four children. Because I was more than five years younger than my next oldest sibling, my childhood had aspects of growing up in a big family combined with aspects of feeling like an only child. My siblings were very good to me and are an important part of what kept me in one piece psychologically.

Shortly after I was born my family moved to Peru. My parents hired a local woman named Eugenia to live with us as a housekeeper and she became, in effect, my nanny, with whom I spent my days while my siblings were at school. As a result I spoke Spanish before I spoke English and spent my early years receiving great love and affection.

Just before I turned three, my family moved back to the United States, and despite Eugenia's efforts to stay in touch, my family gradually dropped out of all contact with her. She had been my primary bond, but I passed the remainder of my upbringing without ever seeing or talking to her again. My parents were mostly kind to me but were distant and unaffectionate people who, for example, didn't even register how traumatized I was by the loss of Eugenia.

My isolation and abandonment left me frequently terrified through my growing years. I was a smart and caring boy, outstanding in school most of the time, and a competent athlete. By the time I finished high school I was pretty well-liked by both kids and adults. And I was terribly emotionally scarred. (And at the same time, I had grown up with great privilege; I would have to say that I'm one of the lucky ones, which just shows what vast stores of emotional injury we're *all* carrying.)

In my late teen years I was plagued by depression and malaise, which led me to explore paths to emotional recovery. Both of my aunts spoke highly of a healing approach they were involved with called co-counseling, which led me when I was 18 to take my first co-counseling class. That summer I unlocked the ability to cry deeply while another person gave me attention, supported me, and held me; and I was also able to open up some other healing channels as well. The result was that almost overnight my life became high energy, joyful, and full of confidence. I was a new person, and everyone around me noticed it. I have never suffered depression again.

In my early 40's a series of twists and turns in my life led me, seemingly out of nowhere, to regain memory of the most important events of my childhood, which I had completely forgotten. I then went through a period of at least five years during which I typically cried hard—not weepy crying, but crying and screaming my guts out like a baby, soaking bandanna after bandanna—for at least an hour *every day*. I emphasize this because the mental health system would have considered me a basket case, in desperate need of medication and probably of confinement, if they had observed what was going on. But any time I wasn't crying during those years—in other words the major portion of each day—I was functioning at a high level and enjoying my life the most I ever had despite facing some of the most painful challenges I ever had.

Those years of doing such powerful and deep healing of my early childhood heartbreak have brought the quality of my life up another tremendous level from the jump it took during my 20's. My commitment to teaching the missing principles of emotional recovery has grown even deeper.

(By the way, I was able to find proof that what I had remembered about my childhood was true; so I now have no doubt that traumatic memories can be completely blocked, and that recovered memories can be largely or even entirely, as turned out to be true in my case, accurate.)

Over the years I've continued to practice the healing approaches I learned as a young man, and to keep studying and exploring other avenues. I have dreamed for a long time of creating a large, inclusive healing network where people can apply certain core principles to supporting each other's recovery. From that drive the Peak Living Network was born in 2017.

From Berkley Books (Penguin Random House):

By Lundy Bancroft

Why Does He Do That?:
Inside the Minds of Angry and Controlling Men

When Dad Hurts Mom:
Helping Your Children Heal the Wounds of Witnessing Abuse

Daily Wisdom for 'Why Does He Do That?':
Encouragement for Women Involved With Angry and Controlling Men

By Lundy Bancroft and JAC Patrissi

Should I Stay or Should I Go:
A Guide to Knowing If Your Relationship Can—and Should—Be Saved

From Sage Publications:

By Lundy Bancroft, Jay Silverman, and Daniel Ritchie

The Batterer as Parent:
Addressing the Impact of Domestic Violence on Family Dynamics